The
IKIGAI
Journey

The
IKIGAI
Journey

A Practical Guide to Finding Happiness
and Purpose the Japanese Way

Héctor García and **Francesc Miralles**

**translated from Spanish by
Russell Calvert**

TUTTLE Publishing
Tokyo | Rutland, Vermont | Singapore

To all those who make the world
a kinder and more beautiful place
by sharing their passions
and awakening those of others.

CONTENTS

How to Awaken the Power of Ikigai

The Ikigai Adventure
A Journey Through the Stations of Happiness

A little over two years ago, the authors of this book completed a project that ended up going much further than we could ever have imagined.

It all started in a Tokyo park where we discussed our shared wish to visit "the village of the centenarians," a rural enclave in the north of Okinawa with the world's longest life expectancy.

We decided to journey to that extraordinary place and there we interviewed the eldest of its residents, who told us their secrets for living such a long, motivated and energetic life.

The outcome of that study was the book *Ikigai: The Japanese Secret to a Long and Happy Life*, which focuses on one of the keys to eternal youth; having a "raison d'être" that can provide us with the happiness that comes from always being busy.

To everybody's surprise, it was the best seller on Spain's most important online bookstore on the very day it was published. Two months later, it had been sold to thirty countries, including the US, Russia, China and even Japan itself.

We got hundreds of messages and letters from readers enthusing about how *Ikigai* had inspired them, but they also asked us: how do I find my ikigai? I know what my life's passion is, but I am always so busy with my responsibilities I hardly have time for my ikigai. How can I realize my dream?

We authors have asked ourselves the same questions. For that reason, we resolved that our next project would be entirely practical and would help both ourselves and our readers to find and empower all aspects of our ikigai.

That was the aim. Two years on, the book you are holding is the fruit of that challenge. We are pleased to present you with a tool that can revolutionize your future by helping you understand your past so that you can live your present the way you want to.

In order to whittle the tool into shape, we set off on a new journey across Japan, the country that inspired our first collaboration, in search of essential lessons to make your ikigai the center of your universe and a driving force for change that will enable you to achieve your life mission.

Ikigai

Written 生き甲斐, *ikigai* is a Japanese word that has no exact translation. Ikigai is the meaning of life, the thing that makes you get out of bed each day in eager anticipation.

The word is made by joining *iki*, 生, meaning "life" or "being alive," and *gai*, 甲斐, meaning "what is worthwhile and has value." So, the literal translation would be "that which makes life worth living."

The Japanese believe we all have an ikigai—or even several—inside us, even if we don't yet know it.

The Shinkansen effect

We came across the Shinkansen effect while researching the "Japanese miracle," which took place between 1960 and 1980, when Japan left its post-war devastation behind to become the second largest economy in the world. Up until now, this ground-breaking concept has been used only in engineering and in Japanese companies, but we are convinced we can take advantage of the same principles to accelerate our personal achievements.

Our mission in the first part of this book is to bring the "Japanese miracle" to the personal life of each of our readers and achieve an exponential leap, taking us from the impossible to the possible in each and every realm of our life.

Yet although the Shinkansen effect concept is a fascinating one, not everything in life is about doing things better and faster.

In the journey we are about to undertake, we have developed techniques to make our past fuel our present, and in turn, for our present to light the way to a future in which we accomplish what we set out to do.

In the East they call it accepting the passage of time, because *the only thing that does not change is change itself.* And this point is worth delving into and understanding so that we may take control of where our life is headed and know how past changes have affected us. In this way, we will be ready in the future when our tracks fork and we have to make crucial decisions.

It is essential to accept the passage of time as an opportunity if we want to be happy and pursue our goals.

Our ikigai is very similar to change; it is a constant that is always with us and mutates depending on which life phase we are in. Our "reason for being" is not the same at the age of fifteen as it is at seventy.

It is essential to be in harmony with our ikigai at every stage. Otherwise, we will feel as though we have strayed from our own path and outside forces have taken control of our everyday life.

Our ikigai is like a radio frequency – the better we tune in to it, the more we will feel that our life has meaning.

This is a route map that will help us to stay tuned throughout the inevitable ups and downs of our ever-changing existence, bringing together the past, present and future to achieve personal fulfillment by accomplishing our calling.

Happiness

Lessons   Passion

IKIGAI

The Ikigai Path

With the **Ikigai Path** we seek a balance between our past, present and future in order to achieve complete personal fulfillment, developing our whole talent in order to accomplish our goals.

On our journey through Japan we chose three locations which helped us to divide this book into three main sections:

1. Journey through the FUTURE: TOKYO

In the Japanese capital we will take the bullet train, aiming for the stars while we design our ideal future. What we can achieve in life is limited only by the reach of our imagination. You will find exercises for planning the future to your full potential and will activate your inner *shinkansen*.

2. Journey through the PAST: KYOTO

We will visit this province with a slow train, which will give us time to savor the landscape of tradition and the past. The nostalgia of this train will help us to reflect upon what we have already lived through and to get to know ourselves better. The answer to the Greek maxim "know yourself" largely comes down to how we reacted to the challenges we were faced with in our past. Interpreting experiences in a positive way is both emotionally and mentally healthy. Being aware of our past gives meaning to our life story. Rediscovering the passions we had as children and teenagers gives us clues that are fundamental to identifying our true ikigai.

3. Journey through the PRESENT: ISE

The Ise Grand Shrine is over two thousand years old. Should it belong to the past? The Japanese destroy this historic building every twenty years and then rebuild it. Thus, the Ise Shrine lives in an everlasting present. This tradition will help us to see how unwise it is to allow ourselves to be dragged down by the weight of the past, since we are free to decide what we want to be and do at any time. While strolling through the Ise Shrine, we will also visit temples where we will learn to draw *enso* circles and understand the power that Eastern disciplines like archery have to draw our spirit into the present. We shall also see how any kind of art is a marvelous tool for anchoring us in the present and helping us reach a state of flow.

This is not just a book. If you read it carefully and apply the suggestions you will find in it to your everyday life, it will take you to a place that, perhaps up until now, has only existed in your imagination.

Prepare to experience great changes and surprises as you enjoy a new landscape.

Breathe and open your mind. The journey is about to begin. Thank you for coming with us,

HÉCTOR GARCÍA & FRANCESC MIRALLES

PART ONE

A Journey Through Our Future

Tokyo 東京

The Shinkansen effect and other techniques for creating great personal projects and developing the inner discipline to see them through

Our starting point is Shinjuku Station, which is traversed by between three and four million passengers a day and is registered in the *Guinness Book of World Records* as the busiest transport hub in the world.

Shinjuku is the epitome of what Japan is capable of achieving:

The first challenge here is managing to meet someone, since this station has over two hundred exits, and getting it wrong can be disastrous. To make things easier for ourselves we decided to meet in the New York Bar on the 52nd story of the Park Hyatt Hotel, the very place where several scenes from the movie *Lost in Translation* were filmed.

Our table is candlelit and encircled by a large window offering views of Tokyo's never-ending sea of buildings. The cityscape shines and twinkles as though it would like to transform into a starry sky.

A live jazz band is playing Miles Davis.

"Here in Tokyo, don't you get the feeling you're in the future?" asks Francesc as he sips on his Yamazaki whiskey.

"That's one of the reasons why I live here," replies Héctor. "Science fiction and futuristic stuff has always appealed to me."

"But doesn't it get to you? Doesn't this obsession with perfection seem a little inhuman to you?"

"Sometimes, yes, I could spend hours telling you about how smothering it is to work in such a perfectionist business environment, but I like to look on the bright side of things."

"Tell me something positive Héctor... if you had to choose one lesson you've learned from Japan after living here for twelve years, what would it be?"

"*Ganbarimasu!*"

"Tiramisu?" Francesc laughs.

"Not tiramisu! It's pronounced *ganbarimasu* and it means 'trying your hardest to achieve an objective.' It's a word the Japanese use when they're facing a challenge, whether it's personal, or sports, or work related. *Ganbarimasu* means 'never giving up,' and that is what I admire the most about the Japanese."

"They don't give up even if it's a seemingly impossible objective...that Shinkansen effect," adds Francesc.

"For sure, having objectives that seem impossible, or setting ourselves lofty ambitions, is what activates the Shinkansen effect in us. But if we don't combine it with the power of ganbarimasu—the continuous effort—our dreams for the future will fade away and never become reality."

"Get ready to activate your Shinkansen effect, Héctor! On this journey, we're going to finish this book."

"*Ganbarimasu!*"

On leaving the Park Hyatt, we moved on to one of the tiny bars hidden away in the backstreets next to Shinjuku Station.

The neon lights and the constant hustle and bustle here makes it seem as though it is never nighttime. Along with Shibuya, this is one of the Tokyo neighborhoods that never sleeps. A frenzied rhythm with no allowance made for rest, with people forever rushing around trying to get the most out of everything and enjoying themselves as much as possible after work.

In a bar that has room for just three customers, we meet a man who has worked for over forty years for the Tokyo city council. We chat briefly (while a strange young man with two cats in a basket watches us) then he comes with us to another backstreet. After climbing several stories of a filthy building, we end up in an Okinawan restaurant, where a man is playing traditional music on a *sanshin*, a string instrument from the southern islands.

This ambience makes us feel nostalgic about the journey we made to Ogimi to write our previous book, *Ikigai*. This is where our first night in Tokyo ends.

The following day, we climb aboard the legendary bullet train.

The Village of Centenarians

In our previous book, *Ikigai – The Secrets of Japan for a Long and Happy Life*, we told of our adventures in Ogimi, a village with little more than three thousand inhabitants in the north of Okinawa, which is considered the place with the highest life expectancy in the world. Not only do they live a long time, but they also have one of the lowest rates of cancer in Japan, and the same is true of other diseases such as diabetes.

Many scientists have gone to Ogimi to study the locals. We went there with a camera on our shoulder and interviewed more than a hundred old people over the course of a week. We asked them about their daily routines, their diet, their family and friends, and about their secret for a health,y long life.

Of course, we also asked them what their ikigai was.

Living with them, we realized nobody was really retired. They were all busy and many of them were working several jobs.

"Ever since you stopped doing the accounting at the greengrocer's you've started to lose your edge," says Akiko to a ninety-six-year-old friend, scolding him for having relaxed after leaving his job. At the age of ninety-two, Akiko combines her role as head of the neighborhood association with the sale of handmade bags in a village shop. She is still fully active and told us: "If you don't do anything, death comes for you."

One of the conclusions we reached in our investigation was that the village of the centenarians' inhabitants have found their ikigai while never ceasing to be active. Perhaps the greatest secret to longevity is to always keep busy, devoting our time to activities we love.

SHINKANSEN
"Bullet train" thinking

Before the train sets a course towards new horizons, let us look at the origin of the concept around which this adventure revolves. To do so, we will go back in time a quarter of a century to look at a man named Jack Welch.

Maybe you are not familiar with the name of General Electric's chairman from 1982 to 2001, a man considered one of the best executives of the last century. Under his leadership a system was introduced to review employees' objectives and tasks on a quarterly basis, which is still used to this day in most medium-sized and large companies.

His system worked reasonably well until he realized certain departments were starting to become less efficient.

What was going on?

The path of least resistance

On closely observing the operating processes, he realized the employees in the various departments were filling in their quarterly objectives sheet proposing *incremental* improvements and even trivialities. In other words, they would write down easily achievable objectives which they were sure of reaching by making as little effort as possible. What is popularly known as the path of least resistance.

Radical Change

Incremental Changes

Incremental vs Radical Omelette

An incremental change is one that adds a little improvement to something that already exists. For example, whenever it was that the first Spanish cook had the idea of adding sliced fried potatoes to the omelette, he managed to change it into a potato omelette. The omelette already existed, and the incremental improvement came from adding potatoes to it.

The radical improvement took place much earlier, when the first individual decided to break an egg, beat it and fry the result. Something that had not existed until then—the omelette—had been born. Unquestionably this was a culinary revolution.

We have all experienced it sometime; when a project's main objectives have already been achieved, we then relax and do just enough to keep everything working. Let's face it, *we humans are lazy by nature*, but if we want to better ourselves and reach new heights, we have to fight against complacency and lack of vision.

This is not restricted just to business matters. The path of least resistance also thrives in a variety of areas, such as:

- Looking after our body and personal health.
- Our relationship with our partner and/or children.
- Managing friendships and free time.
- Intellectual, artistic and even spiritual goals.

Whether out of laziness or because of the fast pace of our lives, we end up eating and sleeping in the same way, until our body gives us a serious warning, or we become stale with our partner until a crisis is provoked, and so on in all areas of our lives.

From time to time we make little adjustments and improvements, like the employees with their quarterly reviews, but they are just band-aids that fail to change the situation in any meaningful way.

It is not always a matter of laziness. Sometimes we are simply busy maintaining what we have devoted so much time to building, and we have neither the time nor the energy to take it to the next level.

Or perhaps true change scares us?

Mikawa's secret

Jack Welch agonized over this problem, which is so typical of the human condition: how to motivate employees of the divisions that were already working quite well, so that they would take risks and keep on innovating?

He would find the answer on a trip he made to Tokyo in 1993.

On this trip he met Eiji Mikawa, the chairman of General Electric's Japanese subsidiary and a specialist in medical technology.

Welch was impressed by the speed at which they introduced changes, outperforming the rest of General Electric's divisions; the Japanese subsidiary had been launching the best and fastest TAC (computed tomography) machines in the world onto the market for years.

Mikawa explained to Welch the secret that inspired the book you are holding:

"If you want a train to go 10 km/h faster, you just add more horsepower to the engine. But if you need to go from 150 km/h to 300 km/h, you have to think about many other things.

Do we need to change all the tracks and make them wider? Do we have to change the suspension system?

Do we need to make the passenger cars more aerodynamic?

You have to think differently—outside the box. You won't get a new train with a few modifications. You need to start from scratch with a whole new way of thinking." *

A seemingly impossible assignment

To find the origin of this eye-opening concept, we have to go back to the year 1958. In the midst of the post-war economic miracle, the Japanese government issued direct orders to JR (Japan Railways) to find a quicker way to connect Tokyo with Osaka.

A few months later, the JR engineers presented a proposal for a train that would travel at an average speed of 100 km/h. This was a breakneck speed for the time and, had this first project become a reality, it would have resulted in one of the fastest trains in the world.

However, the JR executives' response to the engineers was utterly unexpected:

"We need a train that goes twice as fast."

The engineers were utterly astonished, and said it was absolutely impossible to achieve that; a 200 km/h train belonged to the realm of science-fiction movies.

The executives replied that they could spend as much money as they wanted since the government had given them carte blanche for that *seemingly* impossible project.

---

* From the book *Jack Welch speaks: Wit and Wisdom from the World's Greatest Business Leader.*

The Shinkansen effect

The engineers came back a few months later with a new proposal that implied a comprehensive change in all aspects of the future train. To achieve such an outrageous speed, they would need to:

- Change the shape, height and width of the railway tracks that had been used up until then in Japan.
- Spend a large part of the budget on making tunnels to cross the mountainous area around Mount Fuji.
- Completely redesign the concept of "a train" that people had at that time in order to come up with a lighter and more aerodynamic one and thus overcome air resistance.

Essentially, it would have been enough to carry out one or two improvements to gain 10 km/h, but to double the speed you had to *change everything* and approach this mode of transport with an entirely new way of thinking.

This radical change, this Shinkansen effect, is widely used in engineering and business, but we can also apply to all the "divisions" of our life.

To come back to the engineers' "almost impossible mission," in 1964—just six years after the government had thrown down the challenge—the first bullet train in history was inaugurated for the Tokyo Olympics.

Achieving a milestone that caused astonishment around the world, the *Shinkansen* connected Tokyo to Osaka at more than 200 km/h, cutting down the journey time between the two cities from six hours forty minutes to three hours ten minutes.

The innovations that came about through the development of the first bullet train in history would revolutionize train transportation on the entire planet for decades.

The first step towards that great breakthrough, the benefits of which are still visible today, came about when an entirely new way of thinking was adopted.

Shinkansen: The Bullet Train

The term *shinkansen* (新幹線) literally means "new trunk line." The Japanese word is made up of the characters 新, "new," 幹, "trunk" and 線, "line." At the time of its inauguration, in 1964, the train called Hikari (The Light) covered the new trunk line route between Tokyo and Osaka, becoming the first high-speed train in history, reaching a speed in excess of 200 km/h. Both the Hikari train and the *Shinkansen* line came to be widely known abroad as "the Japanese bullet train."

Shinkansen thinking

Eiji Mikawa was fond of talking about how "bullet train thinking" was applied to everything in his company. For example, if the directors in one of his divisions told him they were planning to reduce costs by five percent, he would ask them to think of ways to reduce them by fifty percent.

Jack Welch was so impressed by Eiji Mikawa's approach that he imported the philosophy and applied it to General Electric, where he asked all his employees and divisions to add "bullet train objectives" to their quarterly reviews.

This is one of the main reasons why General Electric has remained competitive and continues to innovate, even though the company was founded more than a hundred years ago and has hundreds of thousands of employees.

"If you have an objective you think you are going to reach in ten years, the best strategy to make it happen is to think about how you can manage to reach the same objective in one year."

Peter Thiel (Silicon Valley investor)

The companies or people that set "bullet train objectives" tend to end up standing out in our society.

For example, Elon Musk resolved to undertake what was in many people's view the "crazy idea" of building rockets capable of taking off and landing; with his private company Space X he duly accomplished in less than ten years something that NASA had not managed to do in over fifty years of research and development.

Elon Musk has also designed the *hyperloop*, a land transport system that could reach speeds of 1200 km/h and, as a personal bullet train objective, he aims to send the first human to Mars. Will he accomplish it?

And what about you? In which area of your life do you want to apply the Shinkansen effect?

Set Your First Shinkansen Objective

For a dream or aspiration to deserve this label, it has to be *seemingly impossible to achieve*. If you feel you can achieve it relatively easily, it cannot be classed as a "bullet train objective."

Visualizing seemingly impossible goals helps you to think laterally and to get rid of old ideas or processes.

Don't be scared to write down your *Shinkansen* objectives.

Do you want to fly your own helicopter? *Write it down.*

Do you want to travel to Alaska and see the aurora borealis? *Write it down.*

Do you want your family business sales to triple? *Write it down.*

Do you want to direct a film? *Write it down.*

We insist on the writing it down part because the first step to achieving a personal milestone is as simple as writing it down.

Get started now:

My number 1 Shinkansen *objective is:*
Of course, just writing something down is not going to make it happen. Next, write down ten initiatives you will undertake to make it easier for you to accomplish your first bullet train objective. State the action, how you will do it and when you will start:

What you will do   How you will do it   When you will do it

1. _____
2. _____
3. _____
4. _____
5. _____
6. _____
7. _____
8. _____
9. _____
10. _____

For example, if my number 1 *shinkansen* objective is to give a speech in front of a thousand people, my action list could be as follows: buy books on how to speak in public, meet speakers who can give me advice, watch YouTube videos of speakers I admire, record myself practicing on camera and watch myself on the computer screen, prepare a simple talk for some local event with a small audience as practice, join a public speaking course, enroll in theater classes to overcome stage fright...

The Uruguayan coach Mario Reyes recommends specifying *what we will do* in each one of these actions, *how we will do it* and *when we will start*. For example:

What you will do	How you will do it	When you will do it
Read books about public speaking	Ask for guidance in a specialized bookshop	Tomorrow at 2.30 pm on my work break

Once you have specified the ten actions, each one of them with its *what, how* and *when*, sign below this sheet, making a binding commitment to yourself and put it someplace you can see it during your daily routine.

Once signed, there is no turning back.

The bullet train will have started rolling.

MOUNT FUJI

Stretching the boundaries

Our train stops at the peaceful town of Mishima, which announces the upcoming view of Mount Fuji. Will the mountain most revered by the Japanese be visible today, or will it be hidden behind a curtain of mist?

Expert travelers ask for a seat "on the Mount Fuji side" when they book a *Shinkansen* ticket from Tokyo to Kyoto, or vice versa. From these seats they wait impatiently for the imposing spirit-mountain to reveal itself in all its splendor.

However, if the day is not entirely clear, the bullet train will pass within touching distance of this dreamed-about place without our managing to see it. Mount Fuji is always there, as are all the great objectives in our life, but sometimes the worldly mists make them invisible to us.

The Mountain of Immortality

The first written reference to Mount Fuji known to us appears in a tenth century tale. The central character is a young girl named Kaguya, who came from the moon and had rejected the emperor's marriage proposal. One August night ,under a full moon, a great light absorbed Kaguya and the Moon people took her back home. The emperor, who was still in love, wrote a letter to the girl and ordered an army of men to take his words to the summit of Mount Fushi (不, "without," 死, "death"), the closest place to the moon known to the ancient Japanese.

When the soldiers reached the summit, they burned the letter in the hope that the smoke would reach the Moon and the emperor's words could be read by Kaguya. Along with the letter, they also burned the elixir of immortality, since the emperor did not wish to live forever.

The word fushi means "without death" or "immortal." With the passing of time, the pronunciation evolved into fuji (富, "full of, wealth," 士, "soldier"), in reference to the heroic soldiers who climbed up to the summit to take the message to the Moon.

Ever since then it has been said that when Mount Fuji erupts, the smoke transports the emperor's words to our moon to converse with Kaguya, thus representing love and the eternal hope of making the impossible possible.

Sir Rutherford Alcock's adventure

However, the first person known to have climbed to the volcano's snowbound summit was not one of the emperor's soldiers, but a Buddhist monk, in the year 663.

Until that point, reaching the summit had been considered impossible, although with time that 'impossibility' was overcome by more and more people. Still, until the start of the Meiji era, in the nineteenth century, no woman or foreigner had been allowed to climb Fuji, as it was considered a sacred mountain.

The first non-Japanese to reach the white summit was the British diplomat Sir Rutherford Alcock who, accompanied by a group of Japanese guards, led nine British climbers to the peak in 1860.

The Japanese officials told him that it was reckless to go up at the end of November and that he would not make it because the weather conditions made it impossible. What's more, a typhoon was approaching Japan.

When Alcock's group began the ascent, the typhoon was indeed approaching. Some government officials said it was a message from the gods warning foreigners that it was a forbidden place for them. But the diplomat ignored everyone who told him it was impossible and, one step at a time, reached the summit, becoming, along with his group, the first foreigner to do so.

At that time, it was not an easy challenge and many mountaineers had died in the attempt, but the athletic Alcock climbed from sea level up to the summit, at an altitude of 3,776 meters, taking eight hours to get there and another three hours to go back down.

ASCENT OF FUSIYAMA

Sir Rutherford Alcock's hand-drawn illustration of Mount Fuji from his personal diary.

Luck was with him, and the typhoon struck the coast of Shizuoka just as he completed his descent.

Alcock described Mount Fuji as an inhospitable, rocky place that looked as though it did not belong to this planet. As he was a very good artist, he produced the first depiction seen in the West of this sacred place's characteristic silhouette.

He narrated his ascent in letters he sent to the British government over the three years he spent in Japan as not only the first British diplomat, but also the first Briton to live in Japanese territory.

> "The last stretch was the hardest; the ever-increasing fatigue
> worked against us. We frequently stopped to fight against
> the pain in our legs and to get our breath back. Some of us
> thought about going back but we carried on until the final
> step up to the mountaintop, which revealed to us the summit
> crater and the views." SIR RUTHERFORD ALCOCK

Mission: possible

Our life is full of mountains we believe to be forbidden or that we feel incapable of climbing, but the fog that prevents us from seeing the path ahead is usually on the lens through which we are viewing it.

We have to wipe our gaze clean of "impossibilities," as we would a steamed-up window, before setting off on our way to the summit. Because the impossible is, in reality, a mental label, a deceptive filter before our eyes.

Over the course of a lifetime there are many things we irrationally feel unable to carry out, since just thinking about them makes us feel terrifyingly dizzy. We go along mentally building many of these walls and when they finally tumble, we cannot believe they ever caused us so much fear, paralysis and frustration in our life.

There is a very thin mental line dividing the possible from the impossible and the job of the engineer or literary *sherpa*, just to give you two examples, is to help us to cross it.

Walt Disney used to say, "There is nothing more enjoyable than doing the impossible." With that in mind, just for the fun of it, it could be a good weekly objective to do at least one thing we feel ourselves utterly incapable of doing.

Learning Japanese or Hungarian, taking up a sport that seems very difficult, playing the piano without sheet music, exploring an untamed country... or climbing the equivalent of Mount Fuji where we live.

As a good friend's WhatsApp motto has it, everything starts with the re-labelling: MISSION POSSIBLE.

Make A List Of Impossible Ventures That Weren't

A very powerful exercise for sweeping our horizon clean of obstacles, prejudices and things we believe we cannot do, is to remember those "impossible ventures" that turned out not to be so.

We tried this out with the following results:

Francesc's 3 False Impossible Ventures:
1. LEARNING TO SWIM. "Until the age of fourteen I was terrified of water and was convinced I would never manage to cross a swimming pool where I couldn't touch the bottom. It took some time, but I ended up discovering I floated."
2. FINISHING A COLLEGE DEGREE. "Considering I failed four or five school subjects every year, neither I nor my teachers nor anyone else thought I was capable of getting my high school diploma, far less any kind of

degree. When I shook off that prejudice, I managed to do a whole degree course in German."

3. HAVING A GIRLFRIEND. "I also saw that as something impossible until I was twenty-three or twenty-four, since the girls I liked seemed like goddesses or extra-terrestrials to me, and out of my reach. The moment I realized they were like me, with fears, doubts and desires of their own, that aura of impossibility disappeared."

Héctor's 3 False Impossible Ventures:

1. WORKING AT CERN. "When reading books on popular science, I always imagined NASA and CERN as places where only the chosen few could work. It seemed like an impossible dream that would forever live in the realm of my imagination. But in 2004 I was accepted at CERN, where what I had imagined turned into reality."

2. TRAVELING TO JAPAN. "As a child I would open an atlas and Japan seemed one of the most remote places on the planet to me, a faraway exotic country that I would most likely never visit. I have now been living in the Land of the Rising Sun for over twelve years."

3. PUBLISHING A BOOK. "Isaac Asimov was one of the authors I was crazy about as a teenager. I read his biography and I was fascinated to find he had published over four hundred books. At that time, the publishing industry Asimov described seemed like something from another world. Now, our book *Ikigai* has an international audience, and the US edition was published by Penguin, one of the publishing houses that published Asimov."

Whenever you feel incapable of doing something, a very effective practice is to write down your own list of all the things that you had at one time you believed you would never achieve, but ended up managing to do. Sometimes they can be silly inventories, as we have shown, but they help to knock down the walls between you and your confidence.

GANBARIMASU

The power of patience and perseverance

The bullet train we on which we're traveling so smoothly towards Kyoto almost flies over the rails; it is the fruit of thousands of hours of work by engineers who did not give up on a shared dream until they had fulfilled it.

Perseverance is one of the values at the forefront of the Japanese mentality. In many Japanese comics and animated shows, the main character often reveals a childhood in which they demonstrate quite a few shortcomings rather than great abilities, but they have a purpose or objective in life—an ikigai that makes them overcome obstacles and carry on.

Through this personal horizon you will gain wisdom and experience continual self-improvement until you become the hero you set out to be. It is also is far more realistic and achievable than a comic book scenario in which the hero's super powers are innate, and the drive that moves them stems from anger or ambition or a desire for vengeance.

Simple goals lead to great achievements

Another characteristic of Japanese heroes is that their objectives are straightforward, simple and pure; they do not have great ambitions.

A typical manga storyline has the leading character wanting to be a good sushi chef, or the best television presenter in his province, or a realtor. There is even a television series—*Shinkansen Girl*—about the life of the bullet train passenger service attendants and how they always strive to improve the way they serve the customers.

They are simple goals, which anyone can identify with, but persevering even in simple goals leads to achieving great personal milestones.

Along with perseverance, patience is a value the Japanese exercise constantly. But this patience does not mean that they wait for things to happen, as if they are expecting some outside miracle to occur. Rather, they practice patience along with perseverance until they achieve what they set out to do.

> "If you want to heat a rock,
> sit on it for a hundred years."
> JAPANESE PROVERB

Doing it as well as possible

The value of perseverance is ubiquitous in the Japanese language and in many of the expressions used on a daily basis.

One of the first words you learn when you study Japanese is *ganbarimasu*, 頑張ります, which is normally translated as "doing it as well as possible." The first two characters that make up the word are 頑, which means "stubborn" or "tenacious" and 張, which means "stretch" or "expand."

Put together, the meaning would be something along the lines of "stretch and expand my stubbornness/objective as far as possible."

The word *ganbarimasu* is at the heart of the expression *ganbatte kudasai*, which means "do it as well as possible," but could be more literally translated as "be stubborn and determined until you achieve what you aimed to do." It is widely used in sporting circles for mutual encouragement and also in the business world when new challenges are being faced.

The *ganbarimasu* philosophy means not stopping until an objective has been reached.

A 100-year plan

The new Japanese bullet train that will connect Tokyo with Nagoya (286 km) in less than forty minutes will become operational in 2027. And not only is everything planned down to the last detail right up until 2027, but there are already plans to use the same magnetic levitation system to reach Osaka in 2045. Likewise, it has been calculated that by the year 2120 this investment in technology will no longer carry a debt, but will begin to make a profit both for JR (Japan Railways) and for the Japanese government.

A plan of more than 100 years!

Before accelerating our personal bullet train, it is important to be clear what our final destination is and at which stations we will need to call.

The *shinkansen* effect driven by perseverance and *ganbarimasu* may be summarized by this formula:

Patience without action leads to a passive life.
Patience with perseverance leads to us fulfilling our goals.

The Man Who Practices

The Swedish psychologist Anders Ericcson, author, with Robert Pool, of the book *Peak: Secrets from the New Science of Expertise*, points out that Homo Sapiens (the man who knows) should actually be called Homo Exercens (the man who practices), since humans are the only species aware that it is possible to improve through practicing.

However, not all types of practice lead to progress. Ericcson divides them into two typologies:

I. NAÏVE PRACTICE. This type that consists of simply dedicating time to something, indiscriminately. Regardless of how many hours you devote to something, if you do it inefficiently or wrongly, you will not make the progress you hoped for.

II. DELIBERATE PRACTICE. This type has a well-designed plan for reaching your goal. Ericcson recommends three main guidelines for this kind of practice:

1. Define the targets. That way, you will know which steps to take and which direction to go in order to reach your goal.

2. Give it your full attention. This will allow you to adapt to different situations and problems without losing focus.

3. Ask for constant feedback to check that you're on the right track, and if not, make the necessary adjustments.

NOTE: see details and implementation in Chapter 5—Feedback: "How others see us," in which we examine techniques for asking for feedback effectively.

The 10,000-hour rule

Inspired by Ericsson's research, a decade ago, the British journalist Malcolm Gladwell wrote the book *Outliers* in which he asked himself why only some people succeed.

Although genetics, family circumstances and education undoubtedly have their part to play in the path to success,

Gladwell points out that *10,000 hours of practice* are necessary in order to succeed. And to illustrate this he cites two cases of geniuses who met this dedication quota before "blossoming":

1. MOZART. Although he began to compose at the age of seven, and some of his teenage pieces are remarkable, he wrote his great works after he was twenty-one, by which time he had accumulated over 10,000 hours composing, practicing and performing in public.

2. THE BEATLES. They too required these 10,000 hours to finally make it big. A good deal of this practicing was done in Hamburg, where they regularly performed from August 1960 to December 1962 in four different clubs, where they intensively perfected their skills. Upon their return to England, they were ready for success.

> "We are what we do repeatedly."
> ARISTOTLE

Now imagine something new you would like to learn.

Before programming the time you are going to devote to it, let's take a look at Gladwell's summary of the different levels that can be reached depending on how much time is devoted to practice:

a. With 1 hour: we will have a basic introduction to the subject.
b. With 10 hours: we will gain a wider notion of the main concepts.
c. With 100 hours: we reach an intermediate level.
d. With 1,000 hours: we become specialists.
e. With 10,000 hours: we become masters of the subject.

This last level represents excellence and, according to the neuroscientist Daniel Levitin, is the time the brain needs to master a field of human activity.

However, an alternative study carried out at Princeton warns that intensive practice may not lead to success if we do not develop *opportunity-recognizing prowess*, once we have achieved mastery.

If, instead of seeking fame and fortune, the Beatles had carried on rehearsing in a basement upon returning to their hometown, we would probably never have heard of them. Fortunately, they used their 10,000 hours well.

Plan your 10,000 hours

If you have a passion that you are greatly attached to—an ikigai you would like to devote your life to—you can consider attaining mastery through the 10,000 hour rule we discussed in this chapter, but this requires commitment and a plan.

Perseverance—*ganbarimasu*—is essential, but you must decide how many years you can or want to allow yourself to achieve your great objective.

The numbers don't lie:

- 8 hours a day x 5 days a week = 5 years
- 4 hours a day x 5 days a week = 10 years
- 2 hours a day x 5 days a week = 20 years
- 1 hour a day x 5 days a week = 40 years

Attaining mastery in a relatively short time demands total dedication, that is to say, our passion must be our job. However, even if we work in something else, a passion—the practicing of a particular art, sport or object of study—can accompany us happily over a lifetime.

The question is, what passion or *ikigai* motivates me

enough to devote my life to it?

If you still don't have an answer to that, consider the words of the great psychiatrist and neurologist Victor Frankl : "If you don't know what your mission in life is, you already have one—to find it."

NEW HABITS

21 days to change your life

We are going to stop looking out of the window for a minute to turn the spotlight on our everyday life. Which habits govern your life? Which ones bring you closer to your goals and make you feel good? Which ones harm you and drain you of energy?

It is said that humans are "creatures of habit," and it is true that habits are essential for our survival, since they are mechanisms that help us to automatize tasks without constantly having to make decisions. If we had to think about every single move we make during the day, we would end up exhausted.

The Happiness that Comes from Repeating

In his novel *The Unbearable Lightness of Being*, Milan Kundera said, "happiness is the desire to repeat," and that may apply to something as simple as our choice of what to wear each day.

Mark Zuckerberg, the young founder of Facebook, has not changed anything about his attire since he made his first public presentation. He still wears the same gray shirt, the same dark gray sweater and the same type of pants and shoes. As he says: "I want to simplify my life so that I have to make as few decisions as possible other than those which serve my community."

This is a very "Zen" way of simplifying things, which may be inspired by the iconic Steve Jobs, who for years wore the same things in all his public appearances: black turtleneck sweater, jeans and white sneakers.

When his biographer Walter Isaacson asked him about this adherence to a single outfit, Jobs explained that he had become friends with the prestigious designer Issey Miyake, who had already designed the uniforms for the workers at Sony, among many other companies.

Although the Apple staff objected in no uncertain terms to Jobs's idea of supplying them with a factory uniform designed by Miyake, he finally decided to get a uniform for himself. This would be very practical for his daily routine and would also become his "personal hallmark" in his presentations.

Without thinking twice, Steve Jobs asked the Japanese designer to make him a hundred black sweaters in his size. When a surprised Miyake asked him why he wanted so many, Apple´s CEO replied: "This is what I wear. This way, I'll have enough for the rest of my life."

Although in a less radical way, another American who joined the club of those who are happy to repeat was Barack Obama, who dresses almost exclusively in gray or blue suits. When asked about this "lack of imagination" he replied: "I don't want to make decisions about what I eat or how I dress every day because I already have too many decisions to make."

Everyday viruses

Repeating habits that help make life easier brings us serenity and happiness. However, there are also bad habits that make themselves at home inside us, as if they were viruses, and unless we consciously deprogram them, it can be almost impossible to get rid of them.

When bad habits take control of our everyday life, they can send it off the rails. On the other hand, if we replace them with good habits, the train heading for our dreams will pick up speed and we will also free up mental space, which will allow us to be more creative. If we have a mental plan of what we are going to do, progress is assured.

For example, the novelist Haruki Murakami wakes up every day at four in the morning and sits down to write for five or six hours. When he finishes, at around nine or ten, he goes out for a run or goes swimming. He devotes the rest of the day to walking, reading and listening to music, as the mood takes him.

The 21-day rule

Charles Duhigg, a *New York Times* journalist, became interested in habits when he realized that each day at three in the afternoon, he needed to eat a large chocolate cookie, despite the fact he had eaten a good lunch and had problems with obesity.

In theory, he wasn't hungry. Where was that irresistible impulse coming from? In the author's words, "Habits are the subconscious options and invisible decisions that surround us on a daily basis."

In researching the question as to what was driving him and how to alter his behavior, he gathered many successful cases and verified that you need to keep at a new positive routine for twenty-one days in order to cement it. Any new habit begins as a choice, and at the end of this period of repetition, the new habit becomes an automatic pattern.

The first step towards being able to reprogram our mind is to *identify the routine* that makes you do the thing that is not in your best interests. In his own case, Duhigg observed how he was overcome by tiredness every day at three in the afternoon, which he redressed by going down to the cafeteria and buying the chocolate cookie.

The second step is *to experiment with new rewards* in order to instill the new habit. What the NYT journalist really needed was to take a break, and the cookie represented the solution he had unconsciously incorporated into his everyday life. Once he was mindful of that, he replaced the "reward" with a healthier one—leaving his office and stopping by a colleague's desk for a ten-minute chat.

He thus managed to have his break without adding to his weight problem.

To establish the new habit over the twenty-one days, so that it would become a part of his routine, Duhigg would set an alarm for the time the subconscious impulse came upon him. That was the signal for the journalist to leave whatever he was doing and pop out to chat for ten minutes with a workmate. If no one was available, he would go out for a walk.

According to several studies, up to forty percent of the decisions we make throughout the day are routines that our brain recreates repeatedly, and in some cases has been doing for years. They are not meditated acts. If we identify the ones that harm us, replace them with positive ones and make an effort to instill the new habit for twenty-one days, our life will take an almost miraculously qualitative leap forward.

How to introduce a new habit

We have based this exercise on Charles Duhigg's techniques. It is aimed at "cleaning out" our bad habits and quickening our pace as we move towards our goals.

For a deeper exploration of habits and how we can train ourselves to form healthy ones, we recommend reading Duhigg's *The Power of Habit: Why We Do What We Do in Life and Business.*

Let's go to the practical application:

STEP 1 – *Identifying how and when the habit appears:*
- What is the bad habit?

  _____

- At what time does it happen?

  _____

- In which place?

  _____

- Which people are around?

  _____

- What emotions do you feel at that point?

  _____

STEP 2 – *Identifying the reward:*
- What is your reward for carrying out your bad habit?

  _____

- Which healthful habit can you replace it with to get a similar reward?

  _____

For example, if we have the bad habit of eating candy in the middle of the afternoon, we can try replacing it with a fresh carrot or some nuts. If we still don't feel satisfied, we can try going for a walk. Maybe the impulse to eat candy stems from feeling bored or anxious. The only way to know for sure is by testing different substitutes until we hit on one that both makes us feel satisfied and does us no harm.

STEP 3 – *Establishing the routine*
It is very hard to suddenly change a routine, which is why it is important to identify a reward in STEP 2 that is motivating enough for us to make the change happen.

Once we have established how and when the habit appears in STEP 1, and the reward that will replace it in STEP 2, we can move on to establishing the new routine that will help us get rid of the bad habit.

- When I feel like _____,
  what I will do is _____
  because it will give me _____
  _____.

For example: *When I feel like* eating cookies at five in the afternoon, and I feel lonely and bored at home, *what I will do is* go out for a walk to clear my head *because it will give me* the reward of energizing myself and the pleasure of anticipating sitting down later with a good book and a cup of tea.

5th STATION
FEEDBACK
How others see us

Having continuous feedback is one of the fundamental principles of engineering, whether it be for train improvements or for a moon mission. Feedback is the mirror that others show us to reflect our progress.

The scientific method is in fact based on "trial and error"; different solutions are tried out—like Edison when he was looking for the filament for his light bulb—and each failure leads to a new alternative until you finally see the light.

This is also applicable to the design of life itself. We can review each area of our life —relationships, career path, finances, cultural circle, etc.—and rate them individually from 1 to 10, depending on how satisfied we are.

The ones that rank low will require us to improve and adjust them, most likely through changing our habits, as we saw in the previous chapter.

Ask for negative feedback

When they asked Elon Musk—whose drive to innovate was discussed earlier in this book—about the secret of his success, he replied: "Pay attention to other people's opinions…, especially the negative feedback from your family and friends."

Getting or giving feedback is not always easy, since feelings can deceive us. Are you capable of telling a friend, to their face, what they are doing wrong? Are you capable of accepting negative criticism about a job you have devoted months of work to?

Never Give Unsolicited Advice

Often, when we see something in another person's life that's not working, we feel tempted to give our opinion, even though we haven't been asked for it. In most cases, all our initiative does is cause the other person stress, since if they had wanted our advice, they would have asked for it.

What's more, this unsolicited feedback may be perceived as criticism, putting the other person on the defensive and possibly generating resentment.

As far back as a century ago, Dale Carnegie was pointing out that criticism is very rarely welcome, since it attacks a person's self-esteem. He claimed that much more is achieved through a positive stimulus—pointing out what they do well.

In those cases where criticism is necessary, because we have a sense of responsibility towards the other person—an employee, student or child—it is important that before we voice it, we prepare the way with praise that makes the recipient feel loved and valued.

Various studies have calculated that in personal and professional relationships the praise-to-criticism ratio is five to one.

When we receive negative feedback, we react instinctively by running away from it. We have trouble accepting it. Few people take the time to analyze what others tell them.

Of course, there is malicious criticism, which is the product of envy, but when several people point out the same problem or behavior, it is worthwhile to step back, look at things objectively, and take steps to make the needed changes.

If we want to take a qualitative leap forward in what we are doing, asking for negative feedback directly may be a big help. This means asking the right people—those we know will be sincere and will not feel obliged to praise us.

The key to getting useful feedback is *to ask specific questions*. If you ask: "What do you think of my latest photo exhibition?" you will almost certainly get generic answers along the lines of: "I love your photos," or "Beautiful."

You will learn nothing from this kind of reply. But if you ask a specific question: "Which of the exhibit's twenty photos do you find the most bland and soulless?" you will get more precise answers and will know what to improve for the next time, especially if you ask why and listen to the answer carefully.

If you get the feeling they can help you with their feedback, probe for details: "Why do you think it's bland?"

Getting good feedback allows us to make much faster progress developing our passion, our ikigai. In the absence of feedback, we run the risk of ending up lost in a sea of possibilities with our compass changing course every morning.

"Here is a golden rule of ethics: think for a moment whether you prefer to receive undeserved praise or receive no praise at all even though you deserve it."
NASSIM NICHOLAS TALEB

Here are a few keys to getting the kind of feedback that will help you improve your life and get closer to your goals:
- Ask for it from people you admire and who know more about the subject than you do.
- Ignore criticism from people you don't know and who know less about the subject than you do.

- Make the other person feel honored to give you feedback. Give credence to those who help you.
- In order to get specific feedback on a job or project, you can ask these three questions:
  a. Can you tell me what you like the least? I won't be offended.
  b. What do you like the most?
  c. And why do you like it?

If they don't tell you exactly why, then forget it because it is not useful feedback.

The SKS approach: Stop, Keep doing, Start

According to Professor Phil Daniels of Brigham Young University, the three following questions are excellent ways of asking others for feedback.

The objective of these questions invite a fearless, honest response. The first one is very subtle because you are asking indirectly rather than directly what it is you are doing wrong:

1. What should I STOP doing?

_____

2. What should I KEEP doing?

_____

3. What should I START doing?

_____

The information you will get from these three questions will help you to speed up the pace of improvement in all areas of your life: work, personal relationships, hobbies, arts, business, etc. The shortest route to self-progress is to pay attention to negative feedback.

SENPAI

Put a mentor (or two) in your life

As we move forward on our journey, we will connect concepts we have learned from previous stations. In this chapter we will combine the 10,000-hour rule with the gathering of feedback we discussed in the last chapter.

Even if we sit down at the piano every day, the bullet train of our talent will never reach high speed if we only ever play our favorite song, the one we already know we have no trouble playing.

To get the most out of practicing any discipline, we need to explore territories outside of our comfort zone.

If we always ski on the easiest slopes, we will never become Olympic skiers.

To overcome the fears and difficulties that come from stepping outside of our comfort zone—part of what Ericsson calls *deliberate practice*—first-rate continuous feedback will be a big help to us.

Put simply, we need a teacher/mentor/coach who will offer us supervision and advice to help us cross the river.

The *senpai-kohai* relationship
When a new graduate starts to work at a company in Japan, they are always assigned a *senpai* to guide them. The senpai is

not a boss, but rather what we might translate as a "mentor."

Their mission is to transmit to the new employee (*kohai*) all their knowledge and skills about the job they have been doing for years.

The *senpai-kohai* relationship is fundamental for the transmission of knowledge and is a key element in the development of Japanese technology and industry.

Can you imagine being the kohai of an engineer who has been designing engines for Toyota for thirty years? We are sure you would learn more about engines by working alongside him for a year than by earning all the bachelor and master's degrees under the sun.

The Everyday "Senpai" University

When I started working in Japan, I was surprised by how ill-prepared the new employees were when they joined companies, compared to the engineers from foreign universities. Some of the new arrivals didn't even know what HTML (the basic language of webpages) was.

However, over time I realized that although they might start almost from scratch, their capacity to listen and follow the path marked out for them by their senpai allowed them to become first-rate specialists over the years, exceeding anything I could have imagined.

HÉCTOR

Who is your mentor?

When we read about people who became well-known for their genius, we sometimes get the feeling they were born with a talent and suddenly, as if by magic, became the best. But behind every genius there was almost always a master or mentor who guided them.

Mozart's father guided his son from a very early age and by the time he was ten, the child had already surpassed the

10,000 hours of *deliberate practice* under his supervision.

Albert Einstein's first mentor was Max Talmey, an ophthalmologist who ate at the Einsteins' home once a week and started to gift him science books when he was still a child.

Geniuses are not born; they are made. You can be the next genius at any age, if you know how to choose a mentor who is capable of helping you ignite your spark and unleash your full potential.

"Satori Piano"

When I started developing my art therapy, I was looking for levers to make a person's creativity suddenly emerge, like uncorking a bottle of champagne. I had already seen for myself the power of fast writing with students who said they were suffering from writer's block, but who were capable of generating high quality texts in the immediacy of the workshop, and something similar happens with visual arts when you allow yourself to be spontaneous. The best creations emerge when you stop the constant analysis and self-criticism.

Achieving the same thing with the piano, an instrument that seems off-limits to people who have never come into contact with it, seemed like a pipe dream. To push past this preconception, I came up with the idea of the *satori piano* ("abrupt illumination" in Zen), taking Professor Antonio Ortuño's simplified method as the starting point.

The challenge was for any person to be able to play a short piano piece with both hands as early as the first session (which lasted less than one hour) and to play a simple version of Pachelbel's *Canon* by the fourth or fifth session. To achieve that I encouraged them to play on the keyboard without sheet music, setting them small challenges that would give way to bigger ones without their realizing it.

To my amazement, almost all the *satori piano* students managed to play two-handed from the start, and in the space of a month were already playing the songs they liked.

However, the aim of this experiment was never to discover great pianists, although some of them demonstrated the aptitude to be so. The great benefit of this drill is to be found on a psychological level; as soon as a person shows they are capable of doing something that seemed impossible to them an hour earlier, a powerful change starts to be triggered on all levels. All the "impossibilities" are called into question and the person launches themselves naturally towards the next challenge in any area of their life.

On a subconscious level, the message we are sending ourselves would be, for example—if you are playing the piano two-handed, which is something you had never dreamed of being able to do, why shouldn't you be able to achieve other things in life, like giving up smoking? FRANCESC

A good mentor will enable you to take the maximum advantage of every hour of practice by keeping you permanently challenged and highly concentrated. Even when it comes to matters of a personal nature, choosing a good *senpai* will help us take an exponential leap in our life, thus achieving the "shinkansen effect." The right choice will help us be more in tune with our ikigai, and always show us when we are straying from it.

They can be an expert in the subject, a therapist, a coach or consultant; a friend who shares your passion may be a big help too, and you can also guide each other.

Self-coaching techniques

While you are looking for the suitable mentor, there are creative ways to get feedback about what you are doing:

- You can use electronic devices to measure your progress in any type of sport, allowing you to see that you are improving.
- YouTube is ideal for seeing people doing the same thing as you, only better.
- If you admire someone in your discipline, read any interviews they have given and take notes. Absorb everything this person has produced and take it as your starting point.
- Log on to specialized Internet forums, tell people what you are doing and ask questions. You'll be able to quickly tell whose posts are most helpful. Try engaging these participants and ask them how you can make progress.
- If, for example, you want to improve your skills as a translator, practice by translating your favorite novel. Compare the result with the book translator's text. Analyze it sentence by sentence. Why did the translator choose

such and such a word while you chose another?
- Read books by people who have achieved the same goals you are pursuing and read their biographies too.

Template for a "deliberate practice" session

1. *Planning the objective, looking and observing*
   Plan the session objective. If it is something completely new, start by analyzing experts who have already done it and pay attention to their methods. Would you choose theirs over yours? Why?

2. *Practice session*
   During the exercise, focus exclusively on what you are doing. To avoid losing concentration, perhaps try the Pomodoro Technique we explain in Chapter 12.

   If it is a mechanical activity requiring you to improve your body movements, record yourself on camera.

3. *Self-feedback*
   Once the exercise is over, it's time to draw conclusions. How was today's session? How did you feel? Happy? Bored? Distracted? _____

   _____

   _____

   _____

   _____

From 0 (*easy*) to 5 (*difficult*), how would you score the session?

_____

Too easy? Find something more difficult for next time.

4. *Detect the errors so you can correct them*

   What did I get wrong repeatedly? Where did most doubts appear? What do I need to improve?

   _____

   _____

   _____

   _____

If you didn't get anything wrong, what you're doing is not ambitious enough and, as a result, you will not progress.

5. *Write down the doubts that surfaced during the session*

   Decide beforehand who you are going to put your questions to. It may either be on an Internet forum, on social networks, in the consulting room of a professional or with a friend who works in the area that interests you.

Make a note of the questions and of the answers as you get them:

   _____

   _____

   _____

   _____

6. *Points to improve in the following sessions:*

   _____

   _____

   _____

   _____

EMULATING

Discovering, imitating and outdoing

At the start of the book, we talked about the miracle behind the creation of the Japanese bullet train. That miracle stands on the shoulders of the inventor of the first working locomotive. His name was Richard Trevithick.

It was in 1802 when this British engineer built the marvelous machine in a steelworks in Wales. He sold his patent a year later to Samuel Homfray, the owner of the aforementioned steelworks who, on seeing what the machine was capable of, made a bet with another industrialist that the locomotive would tow ten tonnes of iron along 15.7 kilometers of track up to the village of Abercynon.

On 21 February 1804, in the midst of great expectation, five boxcars loaded with iron, with seventy men aboard, were towed to their destination at a speed of a little under four kilometers an hour (unloaded, the machine was capable of reaching twenty-five kilometers an hour). To carry out this feat, the train required four hours and five minutes.

Everything has a beginning and *our capacity to improve what already exists is practically unlimited.* And that applies equally to any personal project, however small or insignificant it may seem to us.

Copying to improve

Benjamin Franklin, who stars in a chapter of this book, practiced a strange intellectual exercise; he would read journal articles and, a few days later, would try to write what he had read, as far as he could remember. Then he compared it to the original text. This method is nothing unusual. Great painters began by copying those they admired and comparing the final result to the original.

10 Things Nobody Told You About Being Creative

Austin Kleon's book *Steal Like an Artist* brings together ten unexpected keys to carrying out any project, and the first one is precisely on the subject of taking a model which you will imitate and outdo:

1. *Steal like an artist.* It is not a matter of plagiarizing, but of taking remarkable examples (whether they be works or people) as a starting point for our own projects.

2. *Don't wait to find out who you are before setting things in motion.* Get started now, with whatever you have, and you will gradually discover your identity, talent and ikigai along the way.

3. *Write the book you would like to read.* What has not been done yet, and that you feel is lacking, may be your life mission.

4. *Use your hands.* We have to distance ourselves from screens to get back to using our best tools. "Computers have robbed us of the feeling that we really do things," says Kleon, "you have to involve your whole body, not just your brain."

5. *Extra projects and hobbies are important.* Pastimes make us happy and can also turn into projects that transform our lives and those of others.

6. *The secret—do a good job and share it.* Passing on your creations (and even your thoughts) to others will enable you to get feedback and good ideas.

7. *We are no longer constrained by geography.* According to Kleon, "traveling makes the world seem new to us and our brain work harder."

8. *Be kind (the world is a little village).* Instead of arguing, channel your energy into a creative purpose.

9. *Be bored (it is the only way to work).* After the "creative high," routine and persistence, as we have seen, are important to carry out and complete the "great idea" you have come up with.

10. *Creativity also means lightening the load.* To combat the excess of information, you have to focus on what is key to your project and leave everything else out.

In Japan, "copying" does not have the negative connotation it has in the West, as long as what you are imitating is adapted or improved.

In fact, the *ukiyo-e* prints, such as Hokusai's famous illustration "The Great Wave of Kanagawa" with Mount Fuji in the background, are copies of an original pattern. The pattern is of no value – it is the reproductions that are valuable.

Many Japanese words that mean "copying" are closer to the concept of "reflection," and the reflection of something can occasionally be even more beautiful than the original.

The value of the ephemeral

In western schools we are taught that the older something is, the more valuable it is. If a church has been standing for four hundred years, it appears in guidebooks, while one that was destroyed in the war and rebuilt fifty years ago will almost certainly go unnoticed.

In Japan, the important thing is the intrinsic beauty of something, and the fact it is a copy or reconstruction of the original is of little import. The whole Japanese education system is based on the repetition of *katas*, which seek to copy a particular pattern.

The Ise Grand Shrine, regarded as the most important Shintoist shrine in the world, is knocked down every twenty years and rebuilt "exactly" the same. This is a tradition that has been carried out since the year 690. We can thus calculate that the Ise temple has been rebuilt over sixty times, with the same architectural design always being "copied."

According to Shintoist thinking, this tradition helps maintain the site's freshness and purity. The rebuilding tradition of the Ise Grand Shrine is not looked favorably upon either by guidebooks or by the committee that decides what should constitute a World Heritage Site, but it is vital to understand the value of that which is ephemeral.

Creating something new through symbiosis

Before the fourth century, Japanese was a non-written language. Instead of creating their own system, the Japanese copied the Chinese writing system based on *hanzi* characters. Obviously, the hanzi were not a perfect fit for their language, so they had to change them for what are known today as *kanji* characters. Two new alphabets even had to be created: *hiragana and katakana.*

Thus did the Japanese "create" their language—they took something that already existed and adapted it to their needs. The same thing occurred with the bullet train that astonished the world during the Tokyo Olympics.

Manga is another curious and noteworthy case. Osamu Tezuka is considered the father of manga and based his style on Disney cartoons, American comics and traditional Japanese drawings.

He not only created a new type of comic from these three ingredients, but also something else; he created a new genre called manga.

As an artform manga could be placed at the epicenter of a triangle formed by comics, animation and novels. Once more, Tezuka allowed himself to be inspired, and adapted what he had seen abroad to his own country's art and way of thinking.

Improving the present

The Japanese are well known for being fast at copying and making improvements. So, if they see a new business opportunity that comes from the United States, they swiftly copy it.

When Starbucks began to set up their first outlets in Japan, they realized there were already tens of cafeteria chains there with a similar business model to theirs. They had been copied! And when 7-Eleven started to invade Japan with twenty-four-hour shops, the Japanese not only copied the distribution model but bought 7-Eleven, which is now a Japanese company.

Once it was in their hands, they improved the company and conquered America with more shops and Japanese products.

Recently, Spanish companies began to successfully export ham, and many restaurants offered menus including Serrano ham. Little by little, *iberiko buta* (イベリコ豚, "Iberian pig") began to be incorporated into traditional Japanese recipes.

Inevitably, *iberiko buta* produced in Japan has already appeared on the scene. It can be bought in any supermarket and is cheaper than Spanish ham. If we look at the label, we will see that it does in fact come from Hokkaido pigs fed on *beriota* (they have also imported the Spanish word "bellota," which means "acorn").

If what happened with whiskey happens with ham, Spanish companies have a reason to be worried. A few years ago, after copying and improving the best Scottish distilleries' processes, the Yamazaki Single Malt Sherry Cask was voted the world's best whiskey by British tasters.

A springboard for bettering yourself

Choose a work that you especially admire, which is related to your skills, like writing, music, drawing or—why not?—even cooking.

Let us imagine, for example, that the work is a novel and that writing comes quite easy to you.

In that case, you would follow these steps:

1. *Examine the last novel that really made an impression on you.* Take notes about which strong points make it so appealing (for example, really surprising dialogues, the beauty of its descriptions, the twists and turns of the plot).

   _____

   _____

   _____

2. *Detect its weak points.* Even masterpieces have aspects which, to our mind, could be improved (for example, parts of the novel which are too slow, transitional chapters, or an ending that seems to tail off). Take note and write them down.

   _____

   _____

   _____

3. *"Import" improvements from other works.* In an exercise of symbiosis, look for works that do not have these weak points and add their good points to the list of characteristics the ideal novel would have.

   _____

   _____

   _____

4. *Start a work with all of these qualities.* Once you have listed the positive characteristics all the novels have between them, use them as a guide for your own project.

   _____

   _____

   _____

Maybe you won't manage to create a great work on your first attempt, but you will have good guidelines to work with and perhaps one day you will improve on the original, or even better, create something completely new from this symbiosis which will inspire others.

Many of the artists who started out by copying have ended up being copied.

YOUR ELEMENT

Through what you don't like,
you'll get to what you do

In *Ikigai* we talked about how important it is to find our passion—that is, an activity that enables us to both flow happily and feel we are of use to the world.

However, in today's society, overloaded as it is with stimuli, pressing matters and responsibilities, it is not easy to know what you really want to devote yourself to. And before we set our bullet train in motion, it is vital that we are clear about where we are headed.

Maybe that is why there are so many brilliant people who lead apathetic lives, out of touch with creativity and the search for the meaning of life.

How can they reconnect with their passion?

Our place in the universe

After the preschool stage, many schools not only fail to encourage their students' creativity, but on occasion even stifle the children's imagination. For kids to be introduced to the arts and to creativity, they have to be enrolled in extracurricular activities, which means a financial burden for the parents and an increased workload for the children.

In 1998 the United Kingdom created a "commission for creativity, education and the economy," led by Sir Ken Robinson, which has helped to change education models, not only in the UK but in other parts of the world as well.

Sir Ken Robinson is highly critical of the education system under which he was taught, regretting the fact that neither primary school, secondary school nor college enabled people to develop their talents and discover what they really wanted to devote themselves to.

His definition of the Element has a lot in common with the diagram that opens our book *Ikigai*, in which passion and effort merge into a single entity.

What you love

PASSION   MISSION

What you are good at   IKIGAI   What the world needs

PROFESSION   VOCATION

What you can be paid for

As Robinson defines it, "The Element is the place where the things we love doing and the things we are good at coincide. I believe it is vital for all of us to find our Element, not just because that will make us feel more satisfied, but also because as the world evolves, the very future of our communities will depend on it."

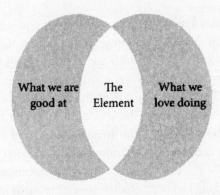

What we are good at | The Element | What we love doing

It is not easy to embark on this search for our place in the universe, and we often find hindrances that make us think of giving up. Not only our own fears and insecurities, but also society itself, which puts obstacles in the way of the brave and punishes those who think differently.

The next horizon

In his recent work *Finding Your Element*, Robinson indicates a series of guidelines to work on the thing we like and lend our talent to making a more creative society:

- Leaving behind your modesty and insecurities, find out once and for all which subjects or skills come naturally to you.
- Change yourself into a confident, responsible person capable of defending and strengthening your abilities.
- Discover what makes you get out of bed in the morning, what fills you with motivation.
- Find out how you can have fun with the thing you adore. For example, building the boat is not the same thing as sailing it.

Once you know what your element is and where to find it, all that remains is for you to set off and enjoy the adventure.

We all know people who are so happy with their job that going to work is just as big a stimulus for them as being on vacation. They might be a firefighter, a teacher or a data analyst— it doesn't matter. The crucial thing is that they have discovered their element and through their hard work they are helping to create a kinder, more generous planet.

This is within everybody's reach. As Robinson says: "Your search will also have its challenges and rewards. Although nobody has lived your life before, there are signs left by many others who set off down this path before you and can guide you. In the end, only you will know if you have arrived or if you have to carry on to the next horizon, if you have found your Element or if you are still looking for it. Whatever the case may be, you must never doubt the search is worth it."

The Negative/Positive test

The creator of psychomagic, Alejandro Jodorowsky, said that if you don't know what you like, start by noticing what you don't like, and through a process of elimination you will get to what you do like.

That is just how this exercise begins:

1. *Write down what you disliked studying.* You can start with subjects you hated at school or in the rest of your education and why.

   _____

   _____

   _____

   _____

2. *Make a list of jobs you loathe.* If you have work experience, write down which ones have made you feel empty or alienated and also specify why.

_____

_____

_____

_____

3. *Make an inventory of the everyday things you really don't like doing.* It may include household chores, organizing your schedule or any day-to-day responsibility that you may find tedious; once again, ask yourself why.

_____

_____

_____

_____

4. *Find the common denominator in everything you dislike.* How are the "stones" in your negative lists similar? Figuring it out will give you a pointer to what you should avoid in the search for your Element.

- *Do repetitive tasks make you weary or, in contrast, does it overwhelm you to do things that require creative thinking or decision-making?*

_____

_____

_____

_____

- *Are they activities you do alone or with somebody else?*

_____

_____

_____

- *Does somebody tell you to do these tasks or do they depend solely on you?*

  _____
  _____
  _____

- *Does it imply a physical or intellectual effort?*

  _____
  _____
  _____

5. *Next, write down everything you like or liked doing in the same categories as before:*
- *School / education*

  _____
  _____
  _____

- *Jobs* _____

  _____
  _____

- *Everyday tasks* _____

  _____
  _____

6. *Find the common denominator in everything you like, with the same questions as in point 4. And add this fifth one: is there a single field or idea that defines your Element?*

  _____
  _____
  _____

7. *Have you stopped doing any of these enjoyable activities? Why did you give it up? What can you do to recover it?*

_____

_____

_____

8. *Make a ranking of the things you love or loved to do. Which would be in first place? How can you give it more prominence in your life?*

_____

_____

_____

9. *Now that what you feel passionately about is becoming clear, ask yourself the key question—what have I always wanted to do and haven't dared to start doing yet?*

_____

_____

_____

10. *Decide how, where and when you are going to start and add a signature to your commitment.*

FRANKLIN

A method for strengthening our virtues

To keep moving forward on our journey, we are going to cast a look back to the eighteenth century to find out about the life of a man who developed his own tools to keep in tune with his ikigai.

Self-reflection and admiration were the two instruments Benjamin Franklin used to go beyond his limits. His biography is eclectic and almost endless; he stood out as a politician, diplomat, inventor and many other things besides, and played crucial roles in the American Revolution and the formation of the United States.

Franklin was also a philosopher and, to use current terminology, devised an interesting method for personal growth.

> "There are three extremely hard things in this world: steel, diamonds and knowing yourself."
> BENJAMIN FRANKLIN

A self-help pioneer

The man who is the subject of this station might be defined as a pioneer of personal growth when this concept, clearly, didn't even exist. And why is that?

This restless American intellectual was already aware that

self-knowledge and imitating those who have progressed beyond us are key to transcending our own limits.

Upon reaching the age of twenty, Franklin set himself a
very ambitious goal—to achieve moral perfection. To do that
he devoted time to reading the biographies of great men who
had gone before him and took from them the virtues he felt
should guide his steps.

Franklin's notebook

The following have come to be known as "Benjamin Franklin's thirteen virtues": temperance, silence, order, resolution,
frugality, industry, sincerity, justice, moderation, cleanliness,
tranquility, chastity and humility.

If we try putting ourselves in his shoes, can we imagine
how a twenty-year-old looking for moral perfection could
stick to following these virtues?

Franklin used cards like the one below to help him. On
the cards he noted the days of the week and qualities needed
to obtain perfection. On a weekly basis he focused on one of
them, putting it at the top of the list, and marked each day that
he had practiced this virtue with the requisite determination.

After thirteen weeks, that is to say, roughly each trimester,
he had finished this series and would start over.

	SUNDAY	MONDAY	TUESDAY	WEDNESDAY	THURSDAY	FRIDAY	SATURDAY
Temperance	✓	✓		✓		✓	
Silence	✓	✓	✓		✓	✓	
Order	✓	✓	✓				
Resolution							
Frugality							
Industry							
Sincerity							
Justice							
Moderation							
Cleanliness							
Tranquility							
Chastity							
Humility							

To take stock of whether or not he had reached the day's goal, he would examine himself at the end of each day. That is, on a daily basis he observed how upright he had been in his search for perfection.

Toward the end of his days, although he knew he had not reached moral perfection, he thought this strict behavioral code and self-awareness routine had made him a better person. To this extent he felt "indebted to his notebook for a lifetime's happiness."

"Human happiness comes not from infrequent pieces of good
fortune, but from the small improvements to daily life."
BENJAMIN FRANKLIN

The thirteen virtues

So, let's take a look at which virtues made the inventor of the lightning rod a wiser, happier, more coherent man. The definitions Franklin associated with each virtue are from the eighteenth century but almost all continue to be relevant today.

1. TEMPERANCE. "Eat not to dullness; drink not to elevation." Unwittingly, Franklin already knew the Japanese *Hara hachi bu* rule – when you are eighty percent full, stop eating.

2. SILENCE. "Speak not but what may benefit others or yourself; avoid trifling conversation." Or as the Japanese proverb puts it: "Whatever you have to say, say it tomorrow." In the final chapter of this book we talk about the importance of the words that come out of our mouths.

3. ORDER. "Let all your things have their places; let each part of your business have its time." In her bestseller *The Life-Changing Magic of Tidying Up*, Marie Kondo stresses how space influences our mental harmony and the development of our ikigai.

4. RESOLUTION. "Resolve to perform what you ought; perform without fail what you resolve." In Chapter 3, where we introduced the concept of *gambarimasu*, we saw how powerful resolve and effort are for any facet of our lives.

5. FRUGALITY. "Make no expense but to do good to others or yourself; i.e., waste nothing." Expressed in modern terms, less is more. Minimalist life encourages us to have fewer things and relationships, but better-quality ones.

6. INDUSTRY. "Lose no time; be always employed in something useful; cut off all unnecessary actions." In Chapter 33, we talk about *kaizen*, the art of incorporating small daily improvements into our lives.

7. SINCERITY. "Use no hurtful deceit; think innocently and justly, and, if you speak, speak accordingly." In the words of Gandhi, "Happiness is when what you think, what you say and what you do are in harmony."

8. JUSTICE. "Wrong none by doing injuries or omitting the benefits that are your duty." The peace of mind that comes from doing what is just avoids weariness that could drain our energy and cost us success.

9. MODERATION. "Avoid extremes; forbear resenting injuries so much as you think they deserve." At the end of the day, outbursts of negativity end up poisoning everyone.

10. CLEANLINESS. "Tolerate no uncleanliness in body, clothes, or habitation." In *A Buddhist Monk's Guide to Housecleaning*, Keisuke Matsumoto points out that all outward cleanliness is at the same time inner cleanliness and thus disperses the clouds of the soul.

11. TRANQUILITY. "Be not disturbed at trifles, or at accidents common or unavoidable." The great Zen master Taisen Deshimaru said that, regardless of the external events, a human's natural state is "silent, peaceful and unagitated."

12. CHASTITY. "Rarely use venery but for health or offspring, never to dullness, weakness, or the injury of your own or another's peace or reputation." Perhaps this is the only non-up-to-date virtue, although it is quite true that enjoying sexuality through deceit is hardly the way to peace of mind.

13. HUMILITY. "Imitate Jesus and Socrates." Enough said.

Create your "Franklin notebook"

To bring this self-improvement method into your everyday life, get yourself a little notebook you can carry with you, or use your cell phone notepad.

Adapting the Franklin method to your own needs:

1. Make a chart like the card we saw earlier, noting the

days of the week and the values you want to develop.

2. Devote each week to developing one of these values and start the day with an intention related to it (for example, to practice gratitude, today I am going to write an e-mail to a former teacher who helped me a lot in my education).

3. If you fail to work on this virtue one particular day, then don't put a check mark in the chart. At the end of the week, you can use it to check how consistent you have been with this objective.

4. When the last week is over, examine the chart and focus on the virtues you have developed the most. If you have seven check marks, that means a virtue has already become an integral part of your life. If you have got few check marks, put this virtue in the chart again so you can practice it again in the coming week.

GASSHUKU

"Shinkansen" sessions

The Japanese believe no one person alone can contribute as much as a gathering of talents. In this culture, the sum of synergies is key, over and above individualisms.

The tasks we carry out alone receive a boost when several talents work together, even if each person tackles their own project. When this this group energy is in play, the lone creator sees him or herself inspired and fueled by the example of others who are pursuing their dreams. A powerful energy comes from sharing space with other people who are operating at fever pitch.

Let's take a look at some of the most famous and surprising examples:

A scary retreat

Two centuries ago, a group of English writers met at Villa Diodati, on the shore of Lake Leman in Geneva. The mansion had been rented by Lord Byron, who invited the poet Percy Bysshe Shelley, who came there with his wife Mary. Byron's personal physician, J. W. Polidori, was also in the house.

The meeting took place in what would come to be known as "the year without summer," due to the violent eruption of the Tambora volcano, in present day Indonesia, which plunged the northern hemisphere into winter during the summer months.

In the midst of this apocalyptic climate, Lord Byron suggested his friends and doctor played a game – each of them would lock themselves in their room until they managed to write a horror story.

Polidori wrote a fragment of what would become *The Vampire*, the first novel of this genre ever written. When they came together to share their writings, Byron's physician should have been the clear winner of the challenge, but he was unlucky. In that very same exercise, it occurred to Mary Wollstonecraft Godwin, Shelley's wife, to come up with nothing less than *Frankenstein*.

She was inspired by the conversations she had heard between her husband and Polidori about the research of the time, in which electricity was applied to corpses to try to reanimate them.

This masterpiece of the genre would probably never have taken shape if all those prolifically imaginative minds had not been shut up together.

"Gasshuku"

"Two weeks from now you have to go to a *gasshuku*," one of our departmental secretaries told me.

She tried to explain to me what a *gasshuku* was, but the only thing I understood was that we were all going on a weekend trip to the Izu Peninsula.

My colleagues and I arrived expectantly at a traditional hotel *(ryokan)*. After dinner on Friday, I eased myself into a hot tub surrounded by bamboo trees from where I had a moonlit view of Mount Fuji.

"If they pay me for this, that's awesome!" I thought grinning from ear to ear.

Saturday came and at five in the morning we were all already up. We ate breakfast in one of the hotel's meeting rooms. Meanwhile the company chairman explained what was expected of us.

The rest of the weekend was a work marathon, without a spare second to bathe in the hot springs with views of Fuji again. On Monday, instead of feeling relaxed after the trip, I was exhausted but felt satisfied. We had generated more ideas and solved more problems over the two days of gasshaku, than in several weeks at the office.

HÉCTOR

A crash course in creativity

In Japanese, the term *gasshuku* is used for the gathering of work colleagues, away from the place they usually meet, with a common objective—to improve by using the whole team's ideas. It is also used for people who study or even practice hobbies together (for example, martial arts). It's what we call an *offsite* meeting, or in engineering circles, a *hackathon*.

We often dream of dedicating more time to our passion, to developing our ikigai, but we are busy with mysterious tasks and routines that somehow always manage to take up all the hours of our everyday life.

But it is not our fault. There are so many pieces in the jigsaw puzzle that makes up our daily routine that we find it hard to make radical changes. We can achieve modest objectives, such as going to drawing class for an hour on Thursdays. There is nothing wrong with going to a school every week, but after three months we will only have devoted twelve hours to drawing.

Can you imagine spending a weekend in a hotel in the mountains with three or four friends who are also fond of drawing, devoting twelve hours a day to landscape painting surrounded by nature?

In just a weekend you would undoubtedly achieve the same results you would get from half a year's effort.

The Novelist's Hotel

In periods when I couldn't concentrate to finish my novels, I began to acquire the habit, when the deadline drew close, of 'confining myself' for several days in a row, sometimes for a week, in a hotel in the city where I lived. One of them, where I finished *Wabi-Sabi*, was so close to home that from my room's window I could see my apartment block.

It was weird seeing my own house while I was typing on my laptop. Being in a place that was both nearby and yet strange stimulated my imagination, while giving me the concentration I needed.

I did more faraway "confinements" in a Montserrat Abbey cell, which I didn't leave until I had finished my thriller *El Cuarto Reino* (*The Fourth Kingdom*).

FRANCESC

Being outside our comfort zone, away from our everyday worries, helps us to concentrate our energies on getting the best out of ourselves and on learning much faster.

It is worthwhile bringing everything to a halt now and again to devote a few days, or at least a fair number of hours at a time, to nurturing our passion.

How to organize "shinkansen sessions"

What they call *gasshuku* in Japan, we call "shinkansen sessions."

SHINKANSEN SESSION: time devoted exclusively to a well-defined, ambitious objective for a continuous period of time, consisting of many hours or even several days avoiding all distractions. Ideally it will be carried out in a place removed from typical everyday lapses of concentration and distractions. The objective is to achieve a qualitative leap forward, as we saw in the first chapter.

Now let's see how to organize a shinkansen session:

- You have to fully commit to the day and time you decide on for the start and finish points.
- Clearly define the objective before starting. Whenever the session starts up, you must be able to work from the get-go.
- Ban cell phones and other means of communication from the starting time right up until the finish time.
- If a lot of people join the shinkansen session, it is best to begin the previous evening, for example, with a dinner or some event to bring everyone together to get to know one another and create a good atmosphere among the attendees.
- To carry out a shinkansen session alone, look for a new place, where you can be separated from distractions. For

example, a country house or even a hotel in your city.

- Remote shinkansen sessions can also be organized with other people who share your passion. The best thing to do in this case is to use collaborative tools such as Skype or Hangout, which allow you to share your computer screen and see each other's faces. It is important for all participants to be fully motivated, so they don't end up side-tracked surfing the Net.

ADVENTURE

Stepping outside your comfort zone

When we take a train toward a new destination, we may at first be stricken by worry upon leaving the world we know. However, after a while, seeing the landscape roll past our window, we are overcome with the calmness typical of travelers who flow with the journey and accept the temporary nature of life.

This willingness of spirit is what must accompany us when we embark upon any adventure, whether it be professional, artistic, or even emotional. We must be aware that we will leave our comfort zone, which will cause us uncertainty, but the new horizons that await us are worth being brave about.

The frog that was boiled alive without knowing it

Our comfort zone is the place or situation where we feel comfortable, because we find ourselves in a well-known environment where we can use our habitual responses, with no need to improvise new solutions or face up to the anxiety of change.

> "The comfort zone is a behavioral state within which a person operates in an anxiety-neutral condition, using a limited set of behaviors to deliver a steady level of performance, usually without a sense of risk."
> ALASDAIR WHITE

However, always remaining in the "known world" prevents us evolving, and many people pay a high price for not abandoning the bosom of what feels comfortable, in the shape of apathy, feeling weary of life, and even depression.

The good news is that challenging our comfort zone is something that comes naturally and instinctively from the moment of birth. It allows us to grow, learn and mature. Children are always venturing into the unknown, until they become adults.

The trouble is that at that point we discover we are vulnerable. We become aware that we have things to lose and that we can get hurt. We stay where we are comfortable. We become like the fabled frog who stays in the pot because, as he becomes accustomed to the slowly rising temperatures, he remains unaware of the danger he's in, and is boiled to death.

Better the devil you don't

None of the breakthroughs that have made society progress would have come about if humanity had remained in its comfort zone.

Likewise, on an individual level, only by venturing into the unknown will we achieve what we really desire. The education and personal growth guru Dale Carnegie puts it this way in *Make Yourself Unforgettable: How to Become the Person Everyone Remembers and No One Can Resist*:

"We learn by doing. Children don't learn to walk by watching others, they try to stand and fall hundreds of times before learning how to put one foot in front of the other in perfect balance. Doing things that are uncomfortable and new ultimately expands your comfort zone. It enables you to confront new tasks courageously—not without fear, but with fear under control."

If you do the thing you think you can't do, you'll feel your resilience, your hope, your dignity, and your courage grow stronger. Someday you'll face harder choices that might require even more courage. When those moments come, and you choose well, your courage will be recognized by the people who matter most to you. When others see you choose to value courage more than fear, they will learn what courage looks like and they will only fear its absence."

We have to put the idea of "better the devil you know" behind us if we want to aspire to something more than survival. We already know our comfort zone inside out. It has already given us everything it can. What if we dare to go a little beyond that?

Short getaways from your comfort zone

Even if your current commitments do not allow you to set off on a great adventure, you can go on some kind of foray outside your comfort zone every day, like a mountaineer who trains in nearby mountains before attacking the highest peak.

You may use these proposals to avoid complacency and to invigorate your everyday life with fresh air:

1. *Change your route to work or to your study center.* Or else change the way you get there. If you usually go by public transport, try biking one day or even walking, if it is not too far, observing the sights you see on the way.

2. *Read a book by an unknown author.* Go into a bookstore and, with no preconceived ideas, allow yourself to be seduced by a cover and a title. At most, read the first paragraph to see how it makes you feel. Maybe you will make the find of the year.

3. *Stroll through a neighborhood where you have never been.* On a non-workday, act like a tourist in your own

town; take the subway or a bus someplace you have never been before. Stroll around the area with "new eyes," observe the buildings and people or go into a bar to soak up the local life.

4. *Learn something new.* However little time you have, join a course in something you have never done: Tai chi, Japanese cooking, calligraphy, drawing models, photography, etc. As well as plunging into a new world, you will come into contact with new people.

5. *Overhaul your friendships.* Particularly if you have put point 4 into practice, open the door to new relationships coming into your life. They will introduce you to different places and you will also renew your topics of conversation. To get new friends, you can also talk to a work colleague with whom you've had a strictly working relationship up until now.

TIMING

Taking each train in time

Do you sometimes have the feeling that the fabric of your life is unraveling around you? Is your appointment book at risk of getting jam packed? Have you had the feeling that your life is about to go off the rails under the weight of all those commitments and responsibilities?

If you have answered "yes" to one or more of these questions, you probably don't have good time management. This often leads to an inefficient management of finances, since time and money are closely linked.

To give a very simple example, if you do not do the shopping in time at the supermarket which has the best offers, you will have to go to the convenience store last thing at night and pay much more.

Now let's see a basic yet efficient method for optimizing your time, money and life.

The comfort zone is a behavioral state within which a person operates in an anxiety-neutral condition, using a limited set of behaviors to deliver a steady level of performance, usually without a sense of risk.

The urgency-importance rule

Organizing yourself well is an art form, and it is often the case that time goes by without our doing half the things we intended to get out of the way before the weekend.

We often have so many things to do that we do not know where to start, and this results in our having a mental block and not carrying out any task at all. Either that or we devote ourselves to something that really is not important, because we think it is urgent.

To better organize our weekly schedule, we need to have a clear idea of which tasks are pressing and, once dealt with, will allow us to enjoy the weekend without feeling guilty and to sleep at night without getting up stressed in the morning.

The objective is to avoid always being behind schedule, so we can act a little like humans from time to time—go to the movies, read a novel purely for pleasure and enjoy other worldly entertainments.

In his talk *The Last Lecture*, Randy Pausch recognized "the Covey matrix" had been a fundamental key to all the successes in his life.

	URGENT	NON-URGENT
IMPORTANT	Time spent on: crises, problems requiring immediate solutions, troubleshooting, deadlines. Results: stress, tiredness, peace of mind. **QUADRANT I**	Time spent on: training, prevention, detecting or creating new opportunities, building relationships, drawing up plans. Results: growth, sound projects, improvement. **QUADRANT II**
UNIMPORTANT	Time spent on: interruptions, phone calls, e-mails, messages, social engagements. Results: fatigue, distraction, lack of concentration. **QUADRANT III**	Time spent on: putting off tasks, unnecessary preparations, social networks, entertainment, enjoyable activities. Results: lethargy, relaxation. **QUADRANT IV**

Following this quadrant, we can make lists with a well-defined order in accordance with the urgency-importance rule. Once we have our task list, we should organize it as follows:

1. We will mark *urgent and important* tasks as absolute priorities and start them as soon as possible.
2. Next, we will take care of the *non-urgent*, important ones.
3. Finally, we will address the *unimportant, urgent* ones.
4. We may simply eliminate the *non-urgent, unimportant* ones from the list.

The Kamprad Method

Ingvar Kamprad, the founder of IKEA, has a "hard" system which suggests the following: "Divide your life into ten-minute units and sacrifice as few of them as possible to meaningless activity."

Three classic ways that time "runs away from us"

Sometimes, we don't know how, but time slips away from us like sand between our fingers. Let's see which are the main "runaways" in modern life and the antidotes we can use to fix them:

- DISTRACTIONS VIA SOCIAL MEDIA. The solution is simple and requires no long-winded explanation—disconnect everything, at least while we are engaged in an activity that requires our attention.
- MEALS WITH FRIENDS AND/OR CLIENTS. A very active professional may find themselves eating in restaurants every day of the week, where, apart from spending money, they "lose" an average of two hours a day. If they also drink wine with the meal, the subsequent drop in performance is tremendous. SOLUTION: accept one or two meals a week at most. If we have to deal with a lot of people, we may group them in fours or fives according to their business area or interests. In that way, we gain work hours and we make a gift of friendships and contacts to others. Another strategy to save time would be to swap the meal for a coffee break that lasts no longer than forty minutes.
- DEALING WITH PERSONAL MATTERS. You should never do this during working hours; if we spend this time on something that should be done during our leisure time, we will find ourselves spending weekends and

evenings—while everyone else is resting—making up for what we should have done.

- Finally, IT IS NEVER A GOOD IDEA TO SKIMP ON SLEEP with the intention of "catching up" later. We may do this very occasionally, for example, the night before the morning of a big delivery, but it should be avoided if at all possible. Apart from the health risks and the risk of speeding up the ageing process, this is not really a way to save time. If you only rest for four or five hours, your mind will work more slowly, and your performance levels will be much lower than if you had rested for at least seven hours. However you look at it, it isn't worth it.

The Pomodoro Technique

A very efficient way of improving your performance and finishing things on time is the so-called POMODORO TECHNIQUE:

1. Divide the time allocated to work into unbroken (distraction-free) 25-minute periods.
2. Take a 5-minute break after each 25 minutes of work.
3. After four "Pomodoros" are reached, we may reward ourselves with a longer break of 15 minutes.

This is a very effective method because limiting the time to 25 minutes forces us to fully concentrate in order to fulfill the little mission we have assigned ourselves. We make sure of giving ourselves breaks and, moreover, we alleviate anxiety with the satisfaction that we are completing many pending tasks.

The technique's name comes from the tomato-shaped kitchen timer used for cooking. When used in the office or home, it helps us with the challenge of accomplishing our missions without dying of exhaustion.

PARETO

The 80/20 rule

Also known as the "law of the vital few" or "principle of factor sparsity," this rule was formulated by the Italian economist Vilfredo Pareto, who asserted that 80% of all observable phenomena are attributable to just 20% of all the possible causes.

The starting point was a calculation of the wealth generation in Italy he made in the early twentieth century. Through this macroeconomic exercise he realized 80% of Italy's wealth was produced by 20% of the population.

The Pareto Principle is not a scientifically demonstrated truth, but it can be a very effective tool for focusing our decision making. It is widely used in the business world and also in engineering. For example, 80% of the traffic in cities tends to build up in 20% of the roads. If you want to improve traffic flow, the best thing to do is focus on improving the 20% with the most traffic. In information technology, the principle appears when we realize 80% of bugs are produced by 20% of the source codes and 80% of Internet traffic is mysteriously concentrated in 20% of the servers.

Less is More

Tanaka was an entrepreneur from the restaurant sector who consulted me a few years ago to improve his profits. When I suggested he eliminated 80% of his menu choices to increase sales at his restaurants, he looked at me like I was crazy.

He told me he didn't want to eliminate anything—what he wanted was to add new things to improve the range of choices. I convinced him to try the stripped-down menu in one of his restaurants as a trial run. A week later, Tanaka phoned me, brimming with excitement, to tell me that in the restaurant with the limited menu, sales had risen by 35%.

This businessman ended up changing the menus in all his restaurants for the minimalist version. Tanaka's mentality has changed from one of wanting to add to one of wanting to rule things out. The last time I saw him he asked me: "What else can I cut out of my restaurant business?" The Tanaka case is a clear-cut example of the Pareto Principle.

HÉCTOR

The first step in applying the Pareto Principle is to gather data on the current state of your business, the way you operate and your lifestyle. The second step, once you have identified what you get the most out of is to get rid of or improve what you get the least out of. This second step is very often the most difficult to take because we find it hard to believe things will improve if we get rid of 80% of stuff.

Essentially, 80% of your profit is generated by 20% of your hard work.

Your ikigai, your passion in life, is not part of the 80% of unimportant things you do every day but is part of the essential 20% you enjoy doing the most. Don't get waylaid by the myriad of choices in that time-consuming, energy-sapping 80%; learn to concentrate your energy on the essential things that bring you happiness and awaken your passions to expedite the search for your ikigai.

The Pareto rule in everyday life

The applicability of this rule to other fields has been widely recognized, and many experts have endorsed it with measurements like the following:

- 80% of the world's resources are consumed by 20% of the population.
- 80% of success is down to 20% of the effort made.
- 80% of the music broadcast on the radio comes from 20% of the songs available.
- 80% of our emotions stem from 20% of our experiences.
- 80% of the customers who come into a store only see 20% of the products displayed.

Of course, this is not an exact science, and these proportions are only approximate, but they can help us realize that most profits and tangible benefits are achieved through making the most of a little bit of hard work. So, we can make our life easier and more effective by making a list of the things and the tasks that give us the most satisfaction and which are our greatest problem-solvers.

Tim Ferriss: The Mathematics of Success

In his bestseller *The 4-hour Workweek*, the entrepreneur Tim Ferriss explains step by step, as the title indicates, how to go from a never-ending schedule, from dusk till dawn, to working just four hours a week.

In order to achieve that, on the one hand he used the Pareto Rule to discover which 20% of clients or products were causing him 80% of his problems and which 20% were responsible for his biggest profits. By getting rid of the former and keeping the latter, he managed to multiply his company's profitability since he freed up time he could then devote to finding more clients from the "premium" 20%.

As the entrepreneur Alberto Cabezas says, a company makes real money when it begins to *fire* clients.

Another strategy Tim Ferriss took into account to be more efficient was Parkinson's Law, named after the Briton who formulated it in 1957. It says that a task will take as much time to do as we have available to do it. In other words, the more time we have to do something, the more time we will waste. A way to avoid that is to set yourself time limits and work to stick to them. *The less time you have to do something, the more you will focus on doing what is important and seeing it through, on account of the pressure.* The result will be the same as or better than if you have an indeterminate amount of time to do it and take things too easy.

Other applications from mathematics? Be clear about what you can offer and limit the possibilities. "The more options you offer a client, the more indecision you create, and the fewer orders you will receive," claims Ferriss. If a designer shows three very different book covers to a publisher, the publisher might reject all three because the subconscious message is that the designer's not clear in their own mind, and they transmit this uncertainty to the publisher.

In this regard, Henry Ford found the ideal formula to satisfy his customers when starting out, hampered by the limitations of his recently opened factory: "You can have any color car you like, so long as it's black."

Less is more.

In our everyday life, where we socialize with a multitude of people, both directly and through social networks, it is not easy to stop to think whether or not our social circles are appropriate for us. Oftentimes we feel overwhelmed by people or activities that we find unfulfilling; this is why it is important to take into account the following, in accordance with the Pareto Rule:

- 80% of the time you wear just 20% of the clothes in your closet (*you can donate the clothes you hardly ever wear*).
- 20% of the problems that worry us are important and 80% are superfluous (*so, remove them from the list*).
- 20% of the people around you bring you 80% of your personal satisfaction (*devote more time to this happy minority and gain time for yourself*).
- You only enjoy or feel happy about 20% of the things you do (*make this 20% your ikigai and even try to make it your profession*).

If we take these points into account, it will be easier to focus on what is really important—devoting our time to the people that matter to us, distancing ourselves from everything that undermines our mood, and finding time to do what we really want to.

Are you in your 20% zone?

Being productive and managing your time and energy well is vital to accomplish your objectives and live the life you want. This aim of this simple exercise is for you to check if you are taking advantage of the Pareto Rule in your life:

- Do you carry out the necessary tasks to achieve the objectives you have chosen?
- Do you know how to delegate or get rid of the unnecessary tasks?

- Do you only use as much energy as is necessary to do what you must?
- Do you give your time to the appropriate people in your circle?
- Do you have productive conversations?
- Do you feel satisfied with your social activities?

If you have answered "no" to two or more questions, that means you are still not in your 20% quality zone and should reconsider and be more rigorous at complying with your priorities.

Next, here are some ideas for actions that will help you choose what is essential and get rid of the rest:

- If you are freelance or have a business, which are the 20% of your clients that generate 80% of your sales? Once you identify the 20% of your clients that make you the most money, get rid of the rest and concentrate your energy on looking after that most valuable 20%.
- Which 20% of your possessions do you value the most and use the most in your everyday life? Get rid of the rest! If you can't face the idea, start with one drawer. Take all the objects out of it and, out of every five, you will most likely only use one on a regular basis. Throw the 80% you don't use in the trash or give them away or sell them.
- Which of the people you normally mix with make you feel the happiest? Spend more time with them and distance yourself from the 80% you least enjoy.
- Which 20% of your garments do you wear 80% of the time?
- Out of all of your hobbies, which are the ones that bring you the most satisfaction? Eliminate the rest and focus on delving into the ones that you feel the most passionate about.

THE POWER OF WORDS

Give your projects memorable names

Yubaba, the witch who is the villain of the movie *Sen & Chihiro's Spirited Away*, steals the names of those she wants to enslave so they will work in her hot springs forever.

Chihiro, whose name means "a thousand ghosts," is a ten-year-old girl who is bewitched by Yubaba and forgets her name. But not only does she forget her name, she also forgets what is real and what is not. Her memories disappear, her personality changes and bit by bit she loses her personal identity.

The storyline of this Studio Ghibli classic may seem somewhat philosophical and complex, but language unquestionably makes us human and differentiates us from animals. Dogs do not call each other by their names—we are the ones who give our pets names.

Change Your Old Programs

If you want to change your reality, you have to change your language and banish negative or defeatist expressions, along with those that *disempower* you, because they place decision-making outside your control. In that sense, there are language changes that transform our way of thinking and therefore also change our acts and their consequences.

Let's take a look at some examples of NLP (neuro-linguistic programming):

INSTEAD OF SAYING...	YOU SHOULD SAY...
I'd like to.../ I wish...	I'm going to...
If only I could... / If only I had...	I'm going to...
I don't know...	I'm learning to...
I can't...	I'm on track to ...
I'm happy when...	I'm happy.

The cone of experience

Language was a fundamental evolutionary step that enabled us to externalize what we were thinking. Philosophers debate about whether or not it is possible to think without language. Nobody has reached a definitive conclusion, but what is clear is that language and reality go hand in hand.

When something has a name, it starts to exist in our reality, while if it lacks a name, it fades away in the universe of the abstract and immaterial. For that reason, there are many exercises in this book where we recommend making lists and writing our intentions down in black and white.

The written word has more power than a thousand vague ideas in our head:

A Personal Contract

In our Ikigai Process, a three-session method aimed at people defining their life objectives and managing to make them come true, I devote the third visit to drawing up a contract together. In this, the person commits to carrying out certain activities on a daily, weekly and more long-term basis. At the end of the contract, they put down their signature and I sign next to it as a witness to the agreement.

To reinforce the contract's power, the person will read the commitment they have just made, every morning for the next twenty-one days—the time it takes to instill a new habit. Thus, after carrying out these actions for three weeks, the life change is guaranteed.

Francesc

According to research into our brain, when we perform something actively, it is much easier for us to remember it and thus to translate concrete actions into reality. When we write about doing something, the brain receives the message; it is actually engaged in performing that action.

As we can see in the graph below, we tend to accomplish 70% of what we write, which means the written word is a powerful instrument for making our plans bear fruit.

The Edgar Dale:'s Cone of Learning

People generally remember...
(learning activities)

People are able to...
(learning outcomes)

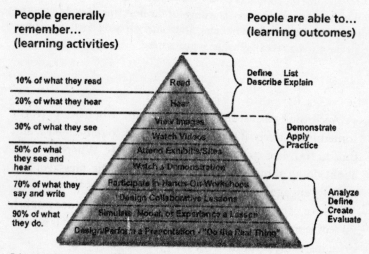

10% of what they read	Define List Describe Explain
20% of what they hear	
30% of what they see	Demonstrate Apply Practice
50% of what they see and hear	
70% of what they say and write	Analyze Define Create Evaluate
90% of what they do.	

Read

Hear

View Images

Watch Videos

Attend Exhibits/Sites

Watch a Demonstration

Participate in Hands-On Workshops

Design Collaborative Lessons

Simulate, Model, or Experience a Lesson

Design/Perform a Presentation - "Do the Real Thing"

When something has a name, it exists forever

If you want to bring your life project into being, baptize it. Choose a sufficiently evocative name to attract you and motivate you to work on it.

As the project progresses, maybe you'll want to change the name because it has evolved toward something else. No problem—change it. What is important is to have something to identify with that allows you to order your ideas and create a story inside you.

In advertising they often talk about "storytelling," the story that lies behind a particular product or company.

And the first page of every story always has a title.

For example, "Nepal Spirit" could be the title of a trip with a couple of friends. We can use the word "spirit" to inspire us and to give the trip a spiritual purpose. If we use this label for all the stages (in the travel preparations, during the trip and then on our return), with the passing of time we will be able to recall those beautiful moments simply by saying: "Do you remember when that monk invited us to spend the night at his temple during the Nepal Spirit…?"

Zeniba, one of the characters who helps Chihiro to get her name back and exist again, says to the heroine: "Once you meet somebody, you never really forget them. It's just that the memory of that person takes a while to come back to you."

Given that our memories are stored in some corner of our inner being, we have to use the right words to evoke hidden memories and connect ideas; they are like springs opening up new universes.

Words are spells with the power to activate memories and neural patterns to make us more creative. For that very reason, it is important to become aware of the power of words.

Find your spell

It is essential for our personal projects to have a name in order to keep us motivated. It is not the same thing to get up in the morning and think you have to go to the gym as to say to yourself: "I'm going to make my Vitruvian Body a reality," in honor of the man to whom Leonardo da Vinci applied the ideal body proportions.

Given that words have power, the exercise we propose is for you to find a spell—a word that resonates strongly with you—to "empower" your projects. Perhaps it could be the name of your favorite band, city, work of art, or the name of a star.

You can even look for a power word for each area of your life you want to improve. For example:

- IMPROVING HEALTH/PHYSICAL FITNESS: "Vitruvian Man Project."
- REVITALIZING LOVE: "Venetian Essence" (if your first romantic trip was there).
- ENHANCING YOUR FINANCES: "Buffett Plan" (if he is your role model—in any case, choose a character you admire in this field).
- WRITING A NOVEL: "Hemingway Session" (for each time you sit down to write, as if you took on the novelist's form).

Use the "power name" as often as you can—say it to your friends and to your partner. And put it in your diary to strengthen your project: "On Tuesday I'm going to create my Vitruvian Body."

PART TWO

A Journey Through Our Past

Kyoto 京都

**Exercises for rediscovering where we come from and
using our personal experiences as a springboard**

From the ancient capital of Japan

In much the same way that history is written by the victors,
each person may interpret their own past positively if they
master themselves. Diving into our origins enables us to bring
our essence and our creativity to the present to build a future
that is full of possibilities.

Nowhere is more of Japan's history preserved than in Kyoto. It was here that Adashi Kakuchi wrote the classic *Heike
Monogatari* in the early fourteenth century.

It is an account of the struggle between the Taira and Min-
amoto clans for control of Japan, interspersed with love stories
and is often compared with Homer's *Iliad*.

Adashi Kakuchi lost his sight when he was thirty years old
and joined a group of musicians in Kyoto that called themselves "The biwa monks" (after a Japanese string instrument)
to make a living. They played music but also recited legends
and war stories—the equivalent of the European troubadours.

Adashi Kakuchi's storytelling technique became so popular
in Kyoto that he became a leading figure in the former capital.

A year before his death at the age of seventy he recited the
Heike Monogatari to his disciple Teiichi, who took on the task

of putting his words down on paper. The novel, which is over eight hundred pages long, can still be purchased today in any bookshop you care to enter in Japan.

If this great epic (where some of the earliest historical events of Japan are played out) was written by a monk who was blind for most of his life…, does it give a faithful rendering of the facts? Probably not, but it doesn't really matter. *Heike Monogatari* is still being published today because it is a story full of beauty.

Beauty always wins. It survives the passing of time. That is why it is worthwhile hanging onto the beautiful things in our life.

After our futuristic bullet train journey out of Tokyo, we have arrived in Kyoto. In the old streets of Gion we can hear a girl playing the *biwa* just as Adashi Kakuchi used to do seven hundred years ago. She is wearing a golden kimono and is kneeling on a tatami opposite screens featuring traditional Japanese drawings. She is not a geisha—not all the girls in Kyoto who wear a kimono are.

She keeps her gaze fixed on the same spot on the ground, some two meters away from her, as if she were meditating. Her fingers flow gracefully and confidently across the biwa strings without a moment's pause, as if they were controlled by supernatural forces. The milky colored skin of her fingers and the pale make-up on her face give her a spooky look that makes us feel as though we have been teleported back to the past in a time machine.

The present and the past are intertwined in an eternal reality.

The spell is broken when the performance finishes and the girl takes out a smartphone she was hiding in her obi, the wide sash cinching her kimono.

Kyoto is the epitome of how the past and the present come together—modernity and tradition dance harmoniously in every corner of this city.

For a complete self-fulfilment, it is also important to be on good terms with our past. Just like Adashi Kakuchi, interpreting our past in a positive and beautiful fashion empowers our present and future and makes our life take on a new meaning.

We have all come out of bad relationships, or misguided work situations or projects that were of no use to us, feeling they had been a waste of time. But we may also choose to think that they did in fact have meaning, and that these apparently negative experiences taught us important lessons for our personal growth.

In this second section of the book, we develop a series of techniques that will help us to explore our past in order to be better writers of the *story of our life*.

"The inevitable death of all things echoes in the ringing of
the Gion Shrine bell."
FIRST LINE OF THE HEIKE MONOGATARI

KINDERGARTEN

Recovering the power of children

Imagine your train now passes by situations from your childhood you had almost forgotten about. You will probably be overcome by a feeling of wistfulness and maybe even sadness. This very emotion sometimes creeps up on us when we contemplate a group of happy children in a park.

Why is that? Could it be that the children's game reminds us of values and dreams we have abandoned by the wayside?

Sometimes getting back what we left behind at kindergarten, before it is too late, is the jolt our life needs.

Watanabe, the star of the movie *Ikiru* (生 きる, "To Live"), one of Akira Kurosawa's masterpieces, discovers he has stomach cancer and that he has less than a year to live. His initial reaction is to meet up with a novelist friend and head out on the town to let himself go in the delights of the Tokyo night. In one of the nightclubs they visit, Watanabe asks the pianist to play "Gondola no Uta" ("The Gondola Song") and starts to sing it himself:

Life is brief,
fall in love,
crimson lips
that fade away
while we are swept up in tides of passion
only to then grow cold,
because there is no tomorrow.

Climb into her gondola,
Before the flush of her cheeks fades away,
for all of you who will come here no more.

Before the gondola gets lost among the waves,
a hand on her shoulder
for those who will not return here.

Before the flame in our hearts
flutters and dies
for those who will never return today.

This song makes him remember how brief life is and how important it is to live it passionately, with an ikigai as a beacon, precisely what Watanabe has not done in all his years devoted to a job he doesn't like.

From that point on, his life takes a new heading. He puts aside his work routine as a bureaucrat and devotes his remaining energy to transforming a waste ground in his neighborhood into a park for children to play in. He dedicates his final months to fighting against the Japanese government bureaucracy to make his childhood dream of a park with swings come true.

The movie ends with Watanabe contemplating the finished park as he again sings "Gondola no Uta."

Reflecting on dreams

Sometimes the great leap forward in our life comes from making what we dreamed of as children come true.

Can you recover those childhood dreams? The first step toward bringing out the best in you may be to put down *everything you wanted to be and do* on a piece of paper.

In fact, what we were passionate about as children contains a lot of clues about who we really are, about our ikigai and our potential as human beings.

A child's mind is free of the bonds imposed by the pressure we see ourselves subjected to once we join adult society. This free spirit is a powerful trigger for creativity.

Just like Watanabe, Randy Pausch, a professor of computer science at Carnegie Mellon University, also got the bad news that cancer was going to take his life earlier than he had anticipated. Pausch's last contribution was to give a lecture entitled "Achieving Your Childhood Dreams."

What he said in that talk made such an impression that it was later published in the book *The Last Lecture*. Randy Pausch explained how much he regretted dying before the age of fifty but how, at the same time, he felt happy and satisfied because he had managed to make his childhood wishes come true.

As well as explaining what those dreams had been about, he proposed that all his students do the same and listen to their inner child so as to believe in the impossible again.

"Think what a better world it would be if we all—the whole
world—had cookies and milk about three o'clock every
afternoon and then lay down with our blankies for a nap. Or
if all governments had as a basic policy to always put things
back where they found them and to clean up their own
mess. And it is still true, no matter how old you are—
when you go out into the world, it is best to hold hands and
stick together."

ROBERT FULGHUM

Going back to pre-school

We do not only abandon dreams among our childhood memories, but also fundamental lessons that end up buried under-
neath the dust of our daily grind and responsibilities.

Like Watanabe in the movie, in 1988 a Seattle teacher realized that *enjoying life and giving free rein to our happiness* may be
the simple secret to being happy and creating the life we want.

Looking back, he recalled the forgotten lessons from kindergarten and school and realized how much help all that
could be to him in his adult life. And that is how he came to
write down his ideas and publish them in his little book *All I
Really Need to Know I Learned in Kindergarten.*

Robert Fulghum never believed his little thesis could become a bestseller with seven million copies sold.

Before graduating with a theology degree and becoming
a teacher, he had done a wide variety of jobs, from digging
ditches to singing country music. But perhaps it was that in-
quisitive spirit or his modest nature that enabled him to redis-
cover his inner child and help many other adults to live with
the powerful energy of their childhoods.

Through short stories starring children, animals and neighbors who are too grown-up, Fulghum teaches us that some of

the most important things we learn in kindergarten are:

- *Share everything.*
- *Play fair.*
- *Put things back where you found them.*
- *Say sorry if you hurt someone.*
- *Live a balanced life, learn something and think about something and draw and paint and sing and dance and play and work a little each day.*
- *When you go out into the world, be careful with the traffic, hold hands and don't go far.*
- *Always pay attention to wonderful stuff. Remember the little seed in the glass: the roots go down, the plant rises, and nobody really knows how or why, but we are all like that.*
- *Goldfish, hamsters and white mice (and even the little seed in the glass) all die.*
- *And so do we.*
- *And then remember one of the first words you learned, the greatest one of all – look!*

In the "look!" of children we can find the seed of what is best about the human spirit, a power that enables us to discover the world, to dream of new adventures and make them come true.

Awaken the child from its slumber

To carry out this exercise, you just need to look back and, holding a notebook, ask yourself the question: *which three childhood dreams have I still not made come true?*

1. _____
2. _____
3. _____

Next, think how you could achieve these dreams. For example, if you wanted to be a movie director and you now work in a publicity agency, you may begin by building up a parallel activity (even if you only devote the weekends to it) in which this dream will have its own space. Maybe you could get some of your colleagues to work with you on your project.

To take these projects from your imagination to reality, at the same time make a note of three things that you can do to make each one of them take shape, along with the launch time:

Dream I

1. _____
2. _____
3. _____

START OF THE ADVENTURE:

_____

_____

Dream II

1. _____
2. _____
3. _____

START OF THE ADVENTURE:

_____

_____

Dream III

1. _____
2. _____
3. _____

START OF THE ADVENTURE:

_____

_____

NOSTALGIA

Returning to the source of our happiness

When questioned about the secret of his buildings' originality, Antoni Gaudí said, "Originality consists of returning to the origin," and a Valencian singer-songwriter completed this idea saying, "Whoever loses their roots loses their identity."

So, a look at who we were (and even at who our ancestors were) may help us to understand who we are, and better still, who we might be.

A basic emotion

Inside Out, one of Pixar's strokes of genius, explains the basic emotions we are born with in a tender and amusing fashion. It also describes how they can give rise to more complex feelings when they join together or mix and are applied to the tough situations we face as we grow up.

Without a shadow of a doubt, sadness is among the most basic emotions. However, it has certain variants which we should know how to recognize, such as melancholy or nostalgia, which may become good, creative allies.

Although it may seem to us that feeling sad is a negative thing, scientists have shown that nostalgia can be beneficial for our health and for the achievement of our objectives, since it makes us recall positive memories and feelings.

Feeling connected to others
"Nostalgic memories are customarily of a social nature, and reviewing these memories increases our perception of being connected to others. In this way, nostalgia is a potent compensatory strategy (...). When people feel alone or excluded, nostalgia helps to restore the sense of connection."
CLAY ROUTLEDGE

As recent research at the University of Southampton shows, nostalgia may even strengthen optimism. In critical moments, the memory of happy, safe moments, as well as of loved ones, helps us to remember that we are capable of reaching our goals, and that we deserve to be loved and valued by others.

So, nostalgia is not only useful for affectionately calling to mind the past, but also helps us to face up to our future, decide what our objectives are, what we want and what we do not want out of life.

A portable happiness reserve

Human beings are so well designed that not only do we come with energy reserves in the shape of fat we can burn, we also have built-in happiness reserves in the shape of pleasant memories that can sustain us when we are feeling downhearted.

The next time you feel sad, powerless or too affected by what is wrong with the world, retrieve one of your life's happy moments. Search for the smell of cinnamon or vanilla that takes you back to your childhood, if that does it for you. Feel yourself in your parents' loving arms again.

Straight away you will see how you feel better, stronger, and willing to be useful to the people around you and kind to them... This is because you will be longing to create new memories that you can call to mind later on with the sweet nostalgia that inspires us to be better people.

Personal archeology

Examine your old photographs, travel souvenirs, personal diaries or simply carry out the exercise of closing your eyes and looking back. Which would be your life's *greatest hits*? At what times have you felt especially happy and fulfilled?

1. _____
2. _____
3. _____
4. _____
5. _____

After unearthing and polishing these happy memories, as an archeologist would do with the pieces they had retrieved, think which project could produce these feelings in you now.

Next, throw yourself into that adventure. Do it for the sake of your future memories.

FRIENDSHIP
Reboot your friend map

In his impressive account *Into Thin Air*, about a disaster experienced on Everest with a group of ill-prepared mountaineers, Jon Krakauer reflects on the importance of choosing your "rope mates" well to avoid ending up being dragged down into the abyss.

This is something we should also be mindful of in our everyday life, which comes with its own hills and cliffs. To develop our ikigai and reach our life aims, it is important to surround ourselves with a circle of trust that can help us to reach our summits and may give us a helping hand at times of peril.

Emotional infection

"We all know people whose energy is contagious after spending a brief moment in their company, and who we feel good to be around, without knowing exactly why. But there are also people who, much to our regret, make us feel depressed, sad and sapped of energy when we socialize with them. These things happen to us because when it comes to our relationships, whenever and whenever we are with somebody, their emotions are catching."

FERRAN RAMON-CORTES

Rope buddies

In order to carry out an *audition* to form the perfect team, we can start by ruling people out. If we want to fulfill our ikigai, these people would be bad "rope buddies":

- Those who are constantly complaining and criticize others (since we will doubtless also be the target of their criticism), thereby infecting us with their negativity.
- Those who take up too much of our time asking for favors or demanding attention.
- Those who tend to let us down when we most need them.

These types of people are easy to recognize because we feel tired, irritated or dispirited after being with them. In other words, we feel worse than before.

The best thing about learning to detect them and progressively push them out of our life is that we free up time that we can then share with a smaller group of friends that "nourish" us more.

Tell Me Who You Spend The Most Time With And I'll Tell You Where You Are

A few decades ago, the American entrepreneur Jim Rohn became famous with a talk based on this idea: "You are the average of the five people you spend the most time with." What he meant with that was our "rope buddies" can gauge our happiness or efficiency level in any area.

In his latest book Álex Rovira mentions this method, which we feel is very helpful for forming a good team to accompany us on our ikigai. Just as the success of an expedition depends on the group's overall virtues and talents, so is our everyday life influenced by the people we spend the most time with.

That is why, according to Jim Rohn, if, for example, we rate the happiness level of the five people we spend the most time with from 1 to 10, their average score will be our very own happiness level. Imagine your "rope" of friends amounts to 9+8+8+2+3 in happiness. The average is 6, which means you live moderately happily. If you wish to "increase your mark," stop making a habit of seeing those who score 2 and 3 and replace them with people with greater vitality. By doing this, you will immediately increase your everyday happiness average.

Ferran Ramon-Cortés, the communication expert and author of reference books such as *La isla de los 5 faros* (*The Island of the Five Lighthouses*), explains that our state of mind depends on the emotions we exchange with others throughout the day.

In his words: "Becoming aware of emotional infection may cause an about-face in our relationships and our life (…). We all prefer to socialize with people who 'charge our batteries' rather than with people who sap our energy. Consciously choosing what we want to pass on will help us maintain better relationships and will provide us with better traveling companions."

The following exercise may help us establish the right priorities in this key area of our life.

How to make a friend map

The first step to understanding our friendships and bringing order to them would be to define the type of relationship we establish with each person, and what this relationship demands of us and does for us.

To better visualize this task, we may fill out these two categories:

1. *Friendships that always or nearly always provide me with optimism and good energy, that make me feel cared about, that inspire trust in me.*

   _____

   _____

   _____

   _____

   _____

2. *People who always or nearly always talk about themselves, who often ask for favors, or whose take on life is nearly always negative; or people I see out of a feeling of obligation, but who I don't feel particularly glad to hang out with.*

   _____

   _____

   _____

   _____

   _____

Once you have separated your social circle into two blocks, now comes the fundamental question:

Which group does each of the five people I spend the most time with belong to?

_____

_____

_____

_____

_____

Next, apply Jim Rohn's exercise to your personal happiness or to the area of your life you want to strengthen. If there is a "fail" that brings your "GPA" down, think about distancing yourself from that person in your circle in order to improve your mark and seek out an "expert" in that field.

HINDSIGHT
Connect the dots

In Steve Jobs's famous talk to Stanford freshmen, the Apple CEO said: "You can't connect the dots looking forward; you can only connect them looking backward. So you have to trust that the dots will somehow connect in your future. You have to trust in something—your gut, destiny, life, karma, whatever. Because believing the dots will connect in the future will give you the self-confidence to follow your heart even when it seems things are not going well. And that is what will make all the difference in your life."

The future is a train and sometimes we do not know where it is taking us. All human beings, without exception, feel doubt and fear when commencing any new life journey, because we do not know if what we are doing today will be of any use or not.

> "Life can only be understood backwards,
> but it must be lived forwards."
> SOREN KIERKEGAARD

Steve Jobs felt lost during his student days and never dreamed that enrolling in calligraphy classes would one day help him to create the best font rendering of any operating system in the market.

His message is that we should not be afraid to follow our instinct as long as we allow ourselves to be guided by our ikigai, the thing that we feel passionate about at each moment of our life.

Even if uncertainty makes us feel dizzy or even causes us to panic, we should trust that everything will make sense in the future. Of course, not everything in life is necessarily useful. Oftentimes we go down dead ends or get it wrong and fail. Even so, when these experiences are seen in perspective, they all become life lessons that will help us to grow as people.

For that matter, having to take a detour to achieve what we want often enables us to admire the most beautiful parts along the way. Many discoveries that we make in places we never expected to be, like Columbus when he came across the Americas, are a much greater prize than the initial objective.

Join the dots from your past

To understand the path you have taken so far and the one you are preparing for the future, start by asking yourself the following questions:

1. *What has the most important event in your life been in the last five years?*

   _____

2. *What happened before that? Which people, which actions on your part and which other dots led to this one of your life events materializing?*

   _____

3. *What happened next?*

   _____

By connecting the answers to the preceding questions, write the story of your last five years, basing it on how the fundamental dots that made your life possible as it is today are joined:

_____
_____
_____
_____

Next, examine how you are creating new dots for your future:

What are you devoting most of your time and effort to right now? Do you know what fruit that will bear in the future?

_____
_____
_____

Is there something you have been wanting to do for some time but don't do because you are afraid of failing or of it being of no use to you?

_____
_____
_____

Try to do the latter for a reasonable amount of time and don't worry if you don't see immediate results. In the end, the dots will join, and everything will make sense.

ANALOG
How to go on a digital diet

Since the economic miracle, Japan has been known for its advanced technology, as demonstrated by the fact that the country managed to make the first bullet train. However, its inhabitants are also enthusiasts of all things done well and like to take the time each thing calls for.

This leads them to seek out activities that allow them to disconnect from the system and slow down the passage of time.

Getting back to film rolls

Cameras that work with rolls of film are still used here. As well as people armed with cell phones and digital cameras, if we take a stroll through Shinjuku Gyoen National Garden, we can also see those who seek the thrill that comes from analog shooting and the beauty of the resultant wait for processing.

Many great Japanese photographers still take photos with cameras from back in the day. And those who have gone over to digital, such as the legendary Daido Moriyama, turn off the screen preview, emulating the experience of shooting with a film-based camera.

Spending a day as a tourist and taking three hundred photos with the cell phone is not the same thing as taking a thirty-six-exposure roll of film that forces you to be selective with where you look.

If a photo doesn't look quite right on a cell phone, you take another ten without thinking about it, with the resultant build-up of "trash" in your folder. With the film roll, you stop to appreciate the place before taking the photo and you think about what you want to capture before springing into action, like a poet before they write a *haiku*.

Analog photography—and manual arts in general—give you time to reflect and enjoy the process. You feel more relaxed and engaged and this will show through in the photo you take.

Anything that helps us to create mental space to free up our creative energies is good for our ikigai.

The example of the fathers of technology

Although technology has made our life much easier and has driven civilization's development, it has also subjected us to and made us dependent on devices, which we sometimes trust in more than in our own feelings.

Many studies show that dependence on new technologies, especially among youngsters hooked on video games and social networks, may be the cause of numerous cases of depression, long periods of absenteeism from work and even suicides. It no longer even surprises us that the first thing most people do when getting up and the last thing they do before going to bed is to look at their cell phone to check for messages.

Few of us take steps to distance ourselves from this new drug, whose adverse effects have led to even the fathers of technology distancing themselves from their own creations. They themselves have recognized the need to get back to the life we enjoyed just a few years ago, by returning to the routine of communicating face to face with the rest of the world.

Even Steve Jobs restricted the use of technology in his home and his children had to wait a long time before being allowed to use the iPad. Chris Anderson, who was the editor of the magazine *Wired* and now runs a drone-making company, assured Nick Bilton of *The New York Times* that he preferred his children to get mad at him rather than let them spend too much time using the very gadgets that he promotes:

"My children accuse my wife and I of being fascists and worrying too much about technology and assure us that none of their friends suffer from the same rules." However, the expert has his reasons for behaving this way, as he declared to the prestigious American newspaper: "We have seen the dangers of technology at first hand. I've seen it in myself and I don't want to see the same thing happen to my children."

The digital diet

Separating ourselves from technology is not easy because it has infiltrated all areas of our life, but *detoxing is possible*. So says another expert in this field—Google's marketing manager Daniel Sieberg.

After developing an intense and award-winning career in television and Internet, this communication guru has experienced for himself the pressure the media can exert on everyday life—not only in the professional sphere but also in our private life: "Despite us regularly questioning what we eat and drink, we rarely ask ourselves what this constant immersion in technology is doing to us. Think about it. Gadgets and webs don't come with nutrition labels. Nobody is regulating the amount of technology you consume or measuring how effective it is for you."

For that reason he wrote the book *The Digital Diet*, based on his personal and work experiences, in which he warns us of the dangers we are subjected to and gives us some pointers to slowly get rid of the excess of technology in our diet.

According to this expert, beginning a healthy digital diet comes down to the following points:

1. Considering the effect technology is having on ourselves and on society. In order to do that, he encourages us to *spend a day or two away from our devices and discover what is going on.*

2. *Studying the amount of technology we use on a daily basis.* That is, analyzing how many devices we have, how often we use them and how much we depend on them.

3. *Reconnecting, little by little, with a controlled use of technology,* which will be complemented by real, close relationships with the people we love.

4. Perfecting the *new technological diet, prioritizing quality over quantity* and enjoying a responsible use, which will improve our quality of life.

The key, according to this expert, is not to spurn technology and get rid of all of our gizmos, but to engage with it, stop considering it a tyrant and make it work for us.

"It's time to make peace with technology, not war. Don't hate your phone, your e-mail or your web services. Adapt them to your routine and tame them in a way that gives you the power. They are at YOUR service."
DANIEL SIEBERG

As with any diet, this one is not suitable for the faint-hearted or the indecisive. But if we follow it and force ourselves to stick to it, we will realize how well it is possible to live in this modern world of ours. And one day we will suddenly find it hard to understand those people who carry on being slaves to a radiation-rich diet.

Analog habits for relaxing
The body and mind

The slowness of analog gives us time to reflect, relax and enjoy the process. Using "slow" technologies from time to time helps our psyche to take a rest from the continuous state of alertness we are subjected to, forever hurrying to answer the vibration in our pocket heralding the latest electronic message.

Here are some ideas to add healthful analog habits to your daily routine:

1. If you only read on electronic readers, buy yourself a printed novel by your favorite author.

2. Do you take notes on a cell phone app? Stop using the phone for that and buy yourself a notepad that fits in your pocket and carry it with you everywhere.

3. Buy yourself an analog camera and use no other camera but this on your next trip. Before taking each photo, breathe in, appreciate and feel the moment and capture this feeling in the photograph. Take the film to be processed and meet with the people who went on the trip with you to have a coffee and look at the printed photos together.

4. Do you work with text on your computer? Print it and check it using a pen. When you review the text on paper, you will come across mistakes you didn't see on the ever-hypnotic screen. New ideas will also occur to you, which didn't emerge while you were working in a rush, keeping an eye out, as you were, for a response to your last e-mail.

5. Buy yourself a record player. Simply having to take the vinyl out of its sleeve and carefully place the needle on it will make you act deliberately and think about the artist you are going to listen to. Also, you can use having to change the record every five or six songs to take breaks as per the "Pomodoro Technique" we saw in Chapter 12.

SLOW LIFE

You can get a long way walking slowly

"Unhooking ourselves" from the technology enslaving us is not enough though to get our natural human rhythm back.

Leaving aside technology for a moment, the modern world is a fast, dizzying place that forces us to cling on tight every day so as not to lose our place. Hurrying is not only commonplace but seems to confer a certain prestige.

The busiest person is seen as the most successful, when it should be the other way around. What use is success and money if you lack the time to savor a cup of tea?

In the face of unjustified rushing about—at the end of the day, we are not being chased by a predator—we have the chance to stop the world and get hold of an easier, more peaceful and pleasurable life for ourselves.

In other words, to enjoy the things we love—our guiding ikigai—it is vital that we recover the simple life and take back control of our life's rhythm.

"I went to the forests because I wished to live deliberately,
to front only the essential facts of life and see if I could not
learn what it had to teach. I wanted to live intensely and
discard everything that was not life... and not, when I came
to die, discover that I had not lived."

H.D. THOREAU, *WALDEN, OR LIFE IN THE WOODS*

Slowness is also modern

It was as early as the nineteenth century that Henry David
Thoreau fled from the civilization that was causing him stress
and spent two years, two months and two days living in a cab-
in in the woods. However, the current Slow Life movement
only began to get organized when many residents of Rome
and several farmers, led by the sociologist and politician Carlo
Petroni, demonstrated against the opening of a well-known
fast food restaurant in the Piazza di Spagna.

Although this and other fast food chains spread all the
same, this was the moment the Slow Food body set out on its
path to becoming a worldwide trend.

At the end of the day, it is all about giving more importance
to quality than to quantity, in all aspects of life:

- Fewer clothes but ones that last longer.
- Less meat but of the naturally farmed kind.
- Fewer tasks and more leisure time.
- Fewer friends but ones who care about us more.
- Making the most of our time for what really matters.

"Our century, which began and has developed under the insig-
nia of industrial civilization, first invented the machine and then
took it as its life model.
We are enslaved by speed and have all succumbed to the same
insidious virus: Fast Life, which disrupts our habits, pervades

the privacy of our homes and forces us to eat fast food.
To be worthy of the name, Homo Sapiens should rid himself of speed before it reduces him to a species in danger of extinction."
OFFICIAL MANIFESTO OF THE SLOW FOOD MOVEMENT

In the end, it is a question of devoting time to ourselves, to our loved ones and to what inspires us.

Enjoying life is a skill we all possess, although we sometimes forget it. "Slow life" allows us to regain control and reconnect with the rhythm of nature.

We just need to opt for a simpler, purer, more satisfying life that is more fun and enjoyable.

Initiatives for joining
The "slow life"

To improve our quality of life exponentially, all we need to do is pay attention to the little things and introduce small changes to our rituals.

Let's see some suggestions:

- Put your phone in airplane mode after a particular time of day.
- Check social networks as little as possible—in a fixed time frame, if you can.
- Choose a single medium and a single time of day for watching or reading the news and focus on the news items that help you live better.
- Favor sustainable and ecological products and clothes.
- Find the time to buy and cook fresh market products and enjoy your dinner table unhurriedly.
- Only spend as much time as absolutely necessary at the workplace but when you are at work, work well.
- Favor physical encounters over virtual ones.

Part Three

A Journey Through Our Present

Ise 伊勢

**Bringing our past and future together
in the eternal present of our lives**

From the main Shintoist shrine

The final days of our journey take us to the coastal town of
Ise. For the Japanese this is Mecca, since the most important of all the Shintoist shrines is to be found here.

We arrive by train and take a taxi to a *ryokan* located
amidst the wilderness. The owner of the traditional lodging
meets us at the door. He opens the trunk of the taxi and helps
us carry our luggage.

"I'm Tanaka," he introduces himself, beaming from ear
to ear.

"Pleased to meet you. I'm Héctor and this is Francesc."

"Oh, you speak Japanese!" he says to Héctor.

"Well, I´m still learning…"

"You´re lucky. You´re in the best ryokan in the area,"
he says, pointing at the seemingly endless wooded horizon,
"the Ise Shrine is located in this forest. It's so close you can
walk there."

The sun sets and the trees take on tones that remind us that
fall is here.

At dawn, we open the window and glimpse the Ise Shrine's
wooden structures peeking out half hidden among the trees

—like living creatures living side by side and in harmony with the nature around them. The *torii* gates' wooden frames encompass what really matters: the trees, the river, the life around it and the *kami* gods that inhabit the place.

We leave the ryokan and plunge into the Ise Shrine universe, which is dedicated to the sun goddess Amaterasu.

We cross the wooden entrance bridge and after going through two torii gates, head into the woods, where the trees are interwoven with the wooden structures dedicated to the gods.

"It's strange – the first time I was here I saw a different shrine, but I get the feeling it's the same one," Héctor remarks, looking at the shrine through one of the torii gates.

"You told me they rebuild it every twenty years," an intrigued Francesc says.

"That's right. The last time they rebuilt it was in 2013. What we're looking at now is the 62nd version. It's been taken down and put up again sixty-two times!"

"In Europe we'd be outraged if we demolished a cathedral only to rebuild it."

"It'd be a lot more expensive. The Ise Shrine is very simple. They use wood from the surrounding forest and don't use any nails or metal parts to reinforce the structure. They follow the traditional construction method and instructions from thousands of years ago. They make the *shimenawa* ropes that mark sacred objects or grounds by twining rice straw. I think that's why it feels like I'm looking at the same thing, even though it's all different. The *essence* is the same."

"As Lampedusa said, "If we want things to stay as they are, things will have to change," Francesc reflects out loud. "This is a kind of eternal present."

Ise has inspired us to write about the present. Meditation is one of the disciplines people most often turn to in order to do this, but the authors of this book believe that any activity that focuses our attention on the present enables us to find the "flow" we referred to in *Ikigai*. Any artistic activity is an excellent vehicle for bringing our spirit and mind into the present, where the greatest achievements are born and major changes are nurtured.

Art always lives in the here and now because it is timeless. Are you ready to flow in a never-ending, happy and creative present?

PRESENCE

If you aim at two ducks, you miss them both

From the train window, a Zen monastery can be discerned, high up on a hillside. It is very similar to the one visited by the stars of *Enlightenment Guaranteed*, the movie released by Doris Dörrie in the year 2000.

This is more of a documentary than a movie, since the actors used their real names and improvised their lines based on a very loosely sketched storyline. Two German brothers, Uwe and Gustav, decide to travel to Japan to get over their respective personal crises and to find themselves in a Zen monastery.

After wandering around lost in Tokyo for a few days, they manage to reach the Sojiji Monastery, where the monks will teach them to devote their whole attention and all their energy to just one thing at a time: meticulously folding a napkin with cutlery, polishing the wooden floor, meditating or reciting mantras.

During filming, the camera simply documented the monks carrying on with their daily routine while the actors joined in.

Multitasking leads to burnout and underperformance

These days distractions have taken control of our lives. Complaining about technological change or turning your back on the advantages it offers is absurd, but what we can do is make decisions so that we are the ones who control technology rather than the other way around.

As we explained in the "Find Flow in Everything You Do" chapter of our book *Ikigai*, numerous studies have shown that *human beings are not efficient multitaskers*. Firstly, because of the limited attention we can devote to each thing. Secondly, because each time we leave a task then go back to it, we suffer greatly from fatigue.

This would explain why we feel exhausted after devoting an hour to multitasking, whereas a gardener or a painter can spend four hours concentrating on the same thing without feeling tired.

Although we might feel we are making better use of our time if we are watching a YouTube video, revising for an exam and answering messages on our cell every fifteen minutes, we would actually make much more progress if we divided our time up into three parts: time for watching YouTube, study time and time for answering messages.

An old hunters' proverb goes: "If you aim at two ducks, you miss them both."

Sitting Down is Zen, Walking is Zen, the iPhone is Zen

Once when I was walking around a temple in the Nagano mountains, I felt transported back to the distant past. I went into a Buddhist temple and saw the monks meditating in a sparsely decorated room.

The meditation session ended and each monk returned to his chores. One of them came out into the garden and sat down on the bench where I was having a green tea. I was amazed to see him take an iPhone out of an inside pocket. He was happy and smiling as he answered the messages. He even let out the odd belly laugh.

Then he put the iPhone back in his pocket, turned to me and asked me my name and where I was from. While I was answering him, he looked into my eyes as if I were the only thing that existed for him in that instant. After this initial conversation, I asked him:

"Doesn't the iPhone distract you when you're practicing Zen?"

"Sitting down is Zen, walking is Zen, the iPhone is Zen. But do not waver."

The monk's reply was a variation of the saying: "Sit down, sit down. Walk, walk. Do not falter."

HÉCTOR

This Zen saying contains the essence of what we call "mindfulness": being present in every moment, feeling our body and our consciousness in whatever we may do.

Whenever we are sitting down, let us devote all our consciousness and body to being seated. Whenever we are walking, let us do the same but concentrating on the act of walking. And the final part, do *not falter*, reminds us of the importance of being fully present in everything we do.

Some ideas to avoid faltering:

- If you are eating, move the cell phone away from the table and do not look at it until you have finished. Even more so if you are eating with others, since they deserve your undivided attention.

- If you are having a stroll, enjoy the walk as if it were the most important thing in the world.
- If you are taking a shower, imagine it is the last one you will ever be able to take in your life. Value each instant the hot water is massaging your body.

Divide your day into time to flow and time to let yourself go

Just as the Zen monk has time to meditate, to answer messages on his cell and to talk with a foreigner, so we too may design our everyday life to include intervals of complete *presence*. In this way, rather than being led by what is urgent, we will be the ones taking control.

A simple technique to achieve this is to put some moments aside for ourselves during the day in order to fully concentrate on one thing.

1st single-flow concentration segment:
Start and finish time: _____
Task: _____
_____
_____

2nd single-flow concentration segment:
Start and finish time: _____
Task: _____
_____
_____

3rd single-flow concentration segment:
Start and finish time: _____
Task: _____
_____

Observations:

- The "Pomodoro Technique" we explained in Chapter 12 may be used in each "flow" segment.
- Let yourself go the rest of the time that falls outside the concentration segments. You don't need to spend the whole day like a Zen monk.

TO WRITE IS TO SELECT
The power of putting pen to paper

Writing is one of the most effective therapies there is. The patients treated by the psychotherapist Shoma Morita (1874-1938), to whom we devote a chapter in *Ikigai*, expressed their emotions on paper every day.

When we allow what is inside of us to come to the surface, not only do we clarify and order our thoughts and emotions, we also clean our subconscious of unnecessary burdens, which helps our life to speed up and head in the right direction.

Medical benefits of writing

Modern science has shown the positive effect writing has on our health. UCLA's Doctor Matthew Lieberman used FMRI (functional magnetic resonance imaging) in his experiment to scan the brains of his subjects, who were divided into two groups:

1) Those who wrote about their emotions every day.
2) Those who either did not practice this habit or only wrote about some neutral issue (such as work reports).

After a few days, amygdala activity among the people in the first group began to drop, which was a physiological sign of good health and low stress.

The study concluded that writing about our life and emotions helps to regulate the amygdala's activity, which in turn regulates the intensity of our emotions.

Creating yourself

"In my diary, I not only express myself more openly to how I would talk to another person – I create myself. My diary is a conduit for my personal identity. It represents me as an emotionally and spiritually free person. So, it is not a simple account of my everyday life. It is something more. In many cases, my diary offers me an alternative."

SUSAN SONTAG

A logbook of your life

The important thing about keeping a diary is that, as its name suggests, you write in it *on a daily basis*. There is no need to do anything sophisticated. Simply...

- Sit down at the beginning or end of the day and write the first thing that comes into your head.
- Write about something exciting that has happened to you today, or about plans for the near future that may be taking shape in your head.
- Try to bring to light the positive side of things.

Regarding this last point, of course we also experience unpleasant things in life. Write about them but ponder what you could have done better to stop them from happening. The fundamental questions are:

1) What have I learned after this bad experience?
2) What changes do I need to carry out in my life for other kinds of things to happen to me?

Create a 5-minute diary

Grab yourself a notepad whose color and design inspires you. If you do not have one to hand, buy one that you will use solely for this mission.

Start a new page every day. Draw a horizontal line through the center.

1) Write for three minutes in the top half straight after waking up in the morning.

2) Write for two minutes in the bottom half before going to bed at night.

Now you have created the sections, let's get to the writing:

In the morning (1 minute for each item):

- Three things I should be grateful for at this point in my life:

  _____

  _____

  _____

- Three things that will make the day that is about to begin special:

  _____

  _____

  _____

- Statement of the day, TODAY I AM GOING TO:

  _____

  _____

  _____

Try not to think too much about what you write. As in the art of *haiku*, which we will see in another chapter, it is about writing the first thing that comes into your head when you open the notebook. The exercise is not called the *5-minute diary* for nothing.

Let's carry on with this express diary:

At night (1 minute per item):

• Three great things that have happened today:

_____

_____

_____

• How could I have made today better?

_____

_____

_____

In the three great things, write the most exciting or significant thing to have happened to you that day. They can be trifles, but things you were not expecting when you woke up that morning. For example: "A friend who hadn't written to me for a year messaged my cell phone and that made me feel loved," or "Strolling through the park, I had a fantastic idea for my next personal project."

When explaining what you could have done to make the day better, you might be tempted to go into lengthy explanations, but it will be much more useful if you are brief, so as to let your subconscious learn while you sleep. It could be something like this: "Today I was swamped with urgent things in the morning. I should have taken control and prioritized the important stuff at the start of the day."

For further information about this technique, seewww.intelligentchange.com/blogs/news/five-minute-journal-tips

HAIKU
Awaken your inner poet

The poet Basho used to say that "*Haiku* is what is happening here and now." This is why these short Japanese poems can be used to express an emotion on paper as though they were paintings or photographs.

In addition to being an art form that activates our very essence, *haiku* is a great tool for self-exploration.

Traditionally, it is composed of three verses with five, seven and five syllables respectively, which aim to be as simple as possible. The verses cannot be overelaborate or contrived, nor can they even be too subjective. The poet's brush strokes must be presented bare, metaphor-free and uncomplicated.

Basho Matsuo (1644-1694) is considered the first great *haiku* master. Through the simplicity of his verses he tackled more complex and traditional types of poetry, like the hundred-verse *renga*. Basho advocated the rejection of artificiality and through his haiku he aimed to find the meaning of life and to be in harmony with nature.

This classic poet was followed by many other Japanese authors, who developed this art form, at times giving it a more descriptive or emotional tone, but without forsaking the spirit of the haiku's brevity.

After the opening up of Meiji-era Japan, the haiku art

form fascinated writers from all over the world, like Jorge Luis Borges, Octavio Paz and Jack Kerouac.

> Petal dance
> Idling wind
> Eternal springtime
> HÉCTOR

How to write a haiku

This book's authors tried their hand at this tiny art form to prove that it is possible to write a haiku in a non-Japanese language while keeping its essence.

In very simple terms, Albert Liebermann's *El Árbol de Los Haikus* (The Tree of Haiku Poems) establishes the following elements which must be taken into account when it comes to writing this kind of poem:

1. It must consist of three verses which do not rhyme.
2. It must be short enough to be read aloud in one breath.
3. Preferably it will include some reference to nature or the seasons.
4. The *haiku* is always written in the present tense (although verbs may be omitted); it never looks into the past or to the future.
5. It must express the poet's observation or astonishment.
6. One of the five senses must be present in the verses.

30 haiku in 30 days

The act of writing a haiku is a magnet that attracts our mind to the present and opens up unexpected places inside us.

We propose that you devote yourself to this art form every day for the next thirty days as an exercise in baring your soul. All you need to do is devote a couple of minutes—the ideal haiku emerges spontaneously, without thinking about it—to writing three verses to express what you are feeling here and now.

You can use a notepad, a notetaking app on your smartphone or even Twitter.

The literary merit of the haiku and where you write it is not so important – what matters is making it a habit over the course of thirty days. Let's take a look at the process:

1. Choose an appropriate time of day, for example, when you are on the way to or from work.

2. Breathe deeply, look around you and ask yourself: what can I see? What can I feel? What can I hear? What can I smell? What is the essence of this moment, within me and around me?

3. After answering this question, don't allow yourself time to think—just write down what has emerged in three brief lines.

After thirty days, read them all.

Can you find any pattern or topic that is repeated? Your *haiku* are probably giving you clues about things you like and value and about where your life is going, but which you have overlooked since you are always too busy thinking about the past and the future.

CRUCIAL DECISIONS

Initiatives that change your life forever

Each day, without exception, we make little decisions that shape our present and affect our future in one way or another. However, some particularly important decisions are especially relevant and change everything. That is why we find it hard to make them.

Leaving a job that is draining us, starting or breaking up from a romantic involvement with someone, changing our profession, city or even country, becoming parents, giving up lifelong habits—each one of these decisions will affect every aspect of our life.

Just as with the bullet train, which made it necessary to change the very concept of what a train was, as we saw in the first chapter, certain decisions are the equivalent of being born again, since nothing will ever be the same as it was before.

> "In adulthood, each person needs to make ten to twelve crucial decisions which will mark their destiny as a human being. A crucial decision is one that means a before and after in your life, since it affects all the areas of your existence."
> JOSEP ANTONI BOLINCHES

A snapshot of your life

Within the crucial decisions category, we would include some which are made by millions of people, like giving up smoking or eating meat, reevaluating one's sexual orientation, ending a marriage, leaving a "steady" job, completely changing one's career, religion or approach to life...

A good measuring rod to know how involved we are in our future would be to consider how many crucial decisions we have made since we first started to hold the reins of our life and how many more we would need to take for our train to reach the destination we wish to reach.

The exercise at the end of this chapter is aimed at visualizing this snapshot—a necessary step towards the accomplishment of our life goals.

How I Got Here

One Saturday evening, after a seminar with Doctor Bolinches, I was thinking about which crucial decisions brought me to where I am now and one of the most important was this one:

- *To never again work in a company.* I made this decision after a very negative experience as an editor. I have stuck to this decision for fifteen years now and have sometimes paid a very high price for it.

Next, I realized that I have recently made new decisions that may be crucial, because they are already transforming my life:

- *Not to sit in front of the computer at night or on the weekend* (apart from the odd e-mail). That was something really ground-breaking for me, because in my first fifteen years as a freelance, I would work from Monday to Sunday and from the morning until bedtime. I didn't even get away from the computer on trips.

- *Never again to beg for anyone's affection.* If someone decides to distance themselves from me, I let them go and stop fighting for their attention, however much we may have shared previously. Within this category, I would include freeing myself from the obligation to always be friendly. It is no big deal if somebody can't stand you—you cannot please everybody.

- *To devote half my working day to people, not to screens.* That is, to take on fewer of the jobs I don't feel like doing and give individualized attention to more people that I can help with the tools I have at my disposal.

- *To make the unconscious conscious.* I came to the conclusion that I had done many things throughout my life that I really didn't want to do. I felt uneasy or worried, but I never asked myself: why do I feel bad doing this? The moment you dare answer that question, the subconscious unease becomes conscious and you can understand it and act accordingly. That is when real change comes.

FRANCESC

It is normal to feel dizzy when making crucial decisions, like anyone else venturing into the unknown, but if you stay where you are, you will sink without having taken a single step.

That is why it is worthwhile analyzing where you are every now and then and detecting the warning signs life sends you, so that you can make the necessary changes to give your ikigai both mental and physical breathing space.

Snapshot of crucial decisions

Start by analyzing your important past decisions, encompassing the moment you managed to take each step and the effect it had on your life. These decisions may be to do with your studies and/or philosophy of life, diet, social life, sexual orientation, priorities, etc. Next, examine the effect each one had on your everyday life.

1. _____
_____

Consequence: _____
_____

2. _____
_____

Consequence: _____
_____

3. _____
_____

Consequence: _____
_____

Carry on listing all the great decisions you recall making and the influence they've had on your life.

Next, record the crucial decisions your life is demanding at this time and the benefits that making them would have. In this way, you will motivate yourself to take the step:

1. _____
_____

Consequence: _____
_____

2. _____
_____

Consequence: _____
_____

3. _____
_____

Consequence: _____
_____

Continue the list until you have written down the most imperative changes.

Even if the sum of the crucial decisions from the past and those you are going to make now does not reach ten, there is absolutely no need to worry. The initiative you take today will bring other big changes in the medium term that will revolutionize your reality.

NIGHT SHIFT
Activating the nighttime office

Each night we journey to unexpected destinations. When we close our eyes, we take an unknown train that carries us through unforeseen settings.

We do not know how our dream world works. It is one of the mysteries of the human mind. But history shows us the relevance of what happens when the nighttime office is activated. Sometimes it even plays a decisive role in our present and future.

Lucid dreaming

Lucid dreams have been a controversial topic for decades among psychology, physiology and neurology experts. Unsurprisingly so, since they allow us to be aware we that are dreaming—and this, in the almost always uncontrollable world of dreams.

Despite the fact that the existence of lucid dreams has been corroborated for some time now by all kinds of testimonies, this phenomenon had not been scientifically proved until a few decades ago.

During a lucid dream, the person who is dreaming is aware they are dreaming, which gives them the rare freedom to explore the corners of their subconscious.

The knowledge that we will not be harmed in any way and so can roam around our dream as we wish opens up to us a world of possibilities. Can you imagine it?

Waking up within a dream

While barely twenty percent of the people are believed to have lucid dreams on a more or less regular basis, there are techniques to induce and improve this cerebral ability which, among many other things, may enable us to find the answers that don't come to us in the waking hours.

This has been demonstrated by the researcher Stephen LaBerge, of Stanford University, one of the pioneers of lucid dream studies, who has devoted most of his career to discovering their ins and outs.

After many experiments and tests with patients, LaBerge was convinced that these dreams may boost our learning ability and, therefore, promote our ikigai even when we are asleep.

In his book *Lucid Dreaming: A Concise Guide to Awakening in Your Dreams and in Your Life* he explains how one of the sleepers he was investigating was able to improve her skills as a hockey player thanks to the lucid dreams she was experiencing, in which she dared to leave her fears and doubts behind her.

The sportswoman subsequently decided to apply what she had learned during the dream to her skating and her ability improved considerably in her waking life.

How to be dreamonauts

Scientists have established that most lucid dreams happen in the REM sleep stage, when there is most brain and physical activity, and that there are two main triggers which bring about oneiric lucidity.

1. Something unexpected or strange happens in the dream (for example, places and things that are not exactly as they are when we are awake), which enables us to realize we are asleep. In this way, we continue in the dream, but are aware we are dreaming and are able to interact with the sleeping mind.

2. When we are woken briefly by some external noise, we quickly fall back into the same dream as before, but this time we are aware we are asleep because we were awake seconds earlier.

When we achieve lucidity, the possibilities are almost infinite, since we can access corners of our mind that we cannot reach consciously in the chaotic, stressful world that surrounds us.

Lucid dreams may help us to overcome fear, train our skills, recover lost knowledge, or even to make decisions and check where they may lead us.

Richard P. Feynman, the winner of the Nobel Prize in Physics, claimed that dream lucidity came to him after a lot of practice and work. For him, as he explained in his memoir *Surely You're Joking, Mr. Feynman!*, the secret lay in being aware of what he was thinking about and of the ideas going around in his head as he allowed himself to fall asleep.

> "....I kept practicing this watching myself as I went to sleep. One night, while I was having a dream, I realized I was observing myself *in* the dream. I had gotten all the way down into the sleep itself!
> RICHARD P. FEYNMAN

Once Feynman had become aware he was dreaming, he could consciously decide how he was going to move around in the dream. It is said that this ability helped him to develop his scientific discoveries.

If you find yourself thinking while dreaming and realize you know you are asleep, don't miss the chance to make the most of those precious minutes. You are inside one of those rare lucid dreams that open the door for you to your most deeply buried knowledge.

And perhaps, the secret to your ikigai is to be found behind one of those doors.

3 Steps for Fostering Lucid Dreams

1. Before going to bed, write or read about the subject you would like to find in the maze of your dreams. If you have some doubt or unresolved problem, leave a written record of it for your nighttime office to work on.

2. A short meditation, even if only to pay attention to your breathing for a few minutes, will help you to enter the dream world more consciously.

3. Have a notebook close by your bed, where you can make a note of your last dream every morning when you wake up. Keeping a record of dream episodes systematically will make you more aware of them and thus help you to detect them through the night. Reading the last dreams in your diary before sleeping will help you in this respect.

ENSO

The circle of inner harmony

We must first discover the nature of our existence if we wish to find our own passion and develop it, as Zen teachings would have it. In order to achieve this, techniques are employed which are aimed at revealing what is hidden inside us: *shodo* (calligraphy), *haiku* (poetry), *koan* (riddles) and meditation.

Drawing the so-called "*enso* circle" is one of the Zen *shodo* techniques for drawing our mind into the present, an essential requirement if we are to flow and be at one with our ikigai.

The technique is at once both simple and difficult to carry out; it involves sketching a circle by hand in one brush stroke while leaving the mind free and uninhibited.

The art of repetition

Japanese calligraphy artists draw this symbol of Japanese minimalism with one stroke; it does not matter if ink drops fall around it. Nor does it matter if it is imperfect.

There are no perfect enso circles. They can be complete or incomplete, but no two are the same. They are all different and unique. According to Japanese *wabi-sabi*, true beauty lies, as in nature, in the imperfect, ephemeral or incomplete.

"The enso circle is a photograph of the mind, a direct pro-
jection of the consciousness. Through enso we can express
much more than with words."

SHO TERAMOTO
(ONE OF THE BEST-KNOWN CALLIGRAPHERS IN JAPAN)

What is important about this experiment is not that you
create better or worse circles. The key lies in how the process
is repeated.

This is commonplace in martial arts—the repetition of
simple movements is the key to making our body and mind at
one with the thing we wish to learn. Before the age of eighteen,
the Japanese have to learn almost two thousand different *kanji*
characters, and the only way to do so is by repeating them.

Having to repeat the same strokes hundreds of times to
learn to write a single character may seem boring or pointless
from our Western viewpoint, as may spending an entire day
drawing enso circles, but this repetition trains our heart in the
art of patience; this is fundamental if we are going to sustain
our ikigai.

They say that you can tell what a person is like from the
enso circle they have drawn. It is a reflection of their personality, a mirror of our *mu*—the empty space or nothingness.

Apparently, Apple's new building, which so happens to be
circular-shaped, was one of Steve Jobs's last ideas and was inspired by enso and his years of Zen practice.

A burglar at the calligrapher's house

Before summing up the spirit of enso in the final exercise, we
shall finish with the story of Ryokan Taigu (1758-1831), a Zen
monk admired by Steve Jobs.

Taigu led a hermit's existence, devoted to poetry and calligraphy. He is considered one of the best Japanese calligraphers of all time and his enso circles hang today in Kyoto museums.

The legend goes that one night the monk came across a thief who had gotten into his home. But the intruder had found nothing of value after searching through the entire house.

Ryokan Taigu said to the thief: "You shouldn't leave empty-handed—take my clothes as a gift."

The thief accepted the clothes and left. The monk then sat down naked and, contemplating the night sky through the window, thought to himself: "Poor thief—if only I could have given him this beautiful moon."

As the night came to an end, Ryokan Taigu took out his paint brush, some Japanese *sumi-e* ink and wrote this *haiku*:

盗人に取り残されし窓の月
ぬすっとに　とりのこされし　まどのつき

The thief left behind the most important thing;
the moon
at my window

How to draw an enso circle

PRELIMINARY NOTE: under no circumstances think about whether or not you are drawing well. Simply let your hand move and draw the circle. It is important to keep your mind clear of rational thought so that your body, arm and hand have the freedom to create.

1. Buy a paintbrush and black ink, or simply use a thick marker. Also get hold of good quality white paper.
2. Before turning your hand to the sketch, breathe deeply once, inhaling and exhaling as much air as you can.

3. Draw the circle with a single stroke. Your hand should not touch the paper, since the movement has to be carried out with the whole arm. *Shodoka* (professional Japanese calligraphers) use their whole body to draw an enso circle. To do that, they draw while kneeling or even standing up.

4. Do not judge it when you see it on paper. The circle can be open or closed, symmetrical or asymmetrical—anyhow it looks is fine!

5. Go on to drawing the next circle.

FINAL NOTE: drawing the enso circle is an activity we may practice as a preamble to another habit to clear our mind of worries. For example, we may do it just before writing in our diary, to get our emotions flowing freely, thus enabling us to express them in writing.

KOAN

The power of lateral thinking

Japanese culture loves winding paths, like the curve in the enso circle. Even for spiritual teachings, the master prefers to use mysterious tools, instead of mantras, so that the pupil reaches a higher plane by him/herself.

One such tool in Zen is the *koan*, a question which aims to confound the student's mind in order to activate their lateral thinking, thereby destroying logical thinking patterns.

These philosophical conundrums can be used to delve into our subconscious with paradoxical questions that stimulate our mind to lead it into *satori*—sudden enlightenment. Given that rational thinking will not bring us solutions, the answer—sometimes as disconcerting as the question—often appears in the student's mind spontaneously.

The so-called *mondo*, like the one that follows, exemplify these peculiar dialogues between master and disciple.

A monk asked his master:
"Which is the path?"
"How pretty this mountain is," the master replied.
"I didn't ask you about the mountain—I asked you about the path," the monk retorted.
"Until you cannot go beyond the mountain, you will not be able to reach the path," replied the master.

A work of introspection

The conversation between the monk and the master may be interpreted in many ways, and we feel the urge to answer back and a desire to continue the conversation with the master.

In Zen monasteries, the master gives the disciple a single *koan*, which he will focus on for days, using it as an object of meditation. There are monks who spend years working on a single koan.

It is not so much about studying as a work of introspection. When the student's lateral thinking—intuition—is activated, he sees the light and then requests a *dokusan* session (consultation with the master). When the conversation is over, if the master considers the disciple to be ready, he assigns him a new koan. Otherwise, he will have to continue with the same one.

According to Zen, logical thinking distances us from the essential nature of the universe.

Lateral Thinking vs Vertical Thinking

"Everybody has found themselves with the typical problem that appears to have no solution until, suddenly, a surprisingly simple solution emerges. Once you have thought of it, the solution turns out to be so obvious you cannot understand why it was so hard to find. Of course, this kind of problem can be difficult to solve if you use vertical thinking.

Lateral thinking does not only focus on resolving the problem; it also takes into account new ways of seeing things and all kinds of new ideas."

EDUARD DE BONO, LATERAL THINKING

Slapping the teacher, moving your hand like a branch swaying in the wind, or tearing up the piece of paper the koan is written on and tossing it to the floor can all be valid responses to a koan.

There is no right or wrong answer; the more creative and less rational the response, the easier it will be for the light to dawn in the disciple's mind.

Some *koans* for beginners

To carry out the exercise in this chapter, this list of questions is a good way to explore the power of lateral thinking:

- What does a one-handed clap sound like?
- Why did your dog bark all night?
- If you meet Buddha, kill him!
- Why doesn't the bird fly?
- What was our original face, before our parents gave birth to us?
- There is plenty of water in the desert. What is the water?
- How can you save a unicorn?

Koan practice

The basic technique for analyzing and studying this tool is as follows:

1. Choose one of the riddles from the list above.
2. Dissect the elements in the koan.
3. Analyze the action it suggests.
4. Let the koan elements and action float freely in your subconscious until an "intuitive answer" comes to the surface. Do not hurry in your search for the answer. The *koan* is like a seed we plant inside ourselves. It will take its time to bloom.

Let the koan dwell in your subconscious for as long as necessary. At times of stress during the day you can use the koan as an object of meditation to bring your mind into the present and let it act like a kind of stress medicine.

Once you have practiced with half a dozen koan, you can create your own during a brainstorming session at work, if you work in a group, or with a group of friends, simply for the pleasure of activating your lateral thinking.

MINDFULNESS

Cultivating your undivided attention

In addition to practicing lateral thinking, *mindfulness* is a very useful technique for working on your ikigai, since it enables us to flow and dig deeper into what we are doing.

Although this concept has come to the West recently, at heart it is a skill which has been practiced in the East for over two thousand years in the various schools of meditation.

Mindfulness, or full attention, is a state of alertness about the present moment in which, calmly and non-judgementally, you are aware of your feelings, sensations, thoughts and body movements. In other words, it is a state in which we are fully aware of the moment, capable of living for the here and now.

As strange as it may seem, it is not a situation we normally find ourselves in. Rushing around, dealing with tasks, being deafened by the noise around us, often lead to our thoughts distracting us from the matter at hand.

"If we are constantly running on autopilot, we will be quite
unaware of the things that matter the most to us.
For example, many people feel sad when they reach fifty or
sixty because they did not pay their children enough
attention when they were little. They were too busy at work
or treated them the same way they were treated,
forgetting how painful that was."

SHARON SALZBERG

Training yourself to live in the present

Concentrating on the present is the best medicine to prevent
the future being full of regrets about the past. And we can
achieve it by practicing giving things our undivided attention.

If you have already found your ikigai, put your five senses
to work on it as if your life depended on it. Leave everything
else out, make your passion your entire universe and forget
about time while you are engaged with it.

If you still haven't found it, focus your attention on the
search. But do it happily, with a playful spirit.

As Mother Teresa said: "Be happy in the moment, that's
enough. Each moment is all we need, not more."

If we become aware of the fact that each moment is unique,
we will not need to carry on looking for happiness.

Master Osho claimed the best training for the present is
to *give yourself up* to a goal-free mental state and abandon all
hope of getting results.

4 Activities for developing mindfulness

1. *The human statue.* Sit down or remain standing, as still
   as possible, to become aware of each part of your body.
   Remaining in a completely motionless state makes you
   pay attention to every muscle in your body.

2. *Five senses, five sensations.* With this exercise you will work on your ability to consciously perceive what is around you. Think of five sensations you can feel, here and now, through each one of your five senses.
3. *Slow race.* This exercise is about doing things as slowly as possible. For example, at mealtimes, take enough time to chew well, savor the flavors of the meal and enjoy what it looks and smells like, as well as the feeling of fullness it gives us.
4. *Say your name to bring yourself back.* This exercise is focused on making you aware of your thoughts. Whenever you realize you are having negative thoughts or are worrying about something or getting side-tracked from the task at hand, call out your name. In so doing, you will get back to the present and realize you were digressing.

SERENDIPITY

When accidents are fortunate

Have you ever thought that some of the best things in life, including discoveries that will mark your life, happen by accident? In this chapter, we are going to talk about serendipity.

The word *serendipity* was first used in the seventeenth century by the British writer Horace Walpole in a letter he wrote to a friend. In it he explained to him how the characters in the Persian fairy tale *The Three Princes of Serendip* were always traveling and making chance discoveries.

But the three princes did not await their luck inside a castle, surrounded by wealth waiting for good things to happen to them. They were brave and wise, never gave up and continued their search for good fortune even when things were not going well.

"Look for something, find something else, and realize that
what you've found is more suited to your needs than what
you thought you were looking for."
Lawrence Block

Serendipity is not magic

In the world of science it is well known that many great discoveries have been made by accident. Perhaps the most famous of them is the discovery of penicillin.

Fleming forgot about a Petri dish he had left in the laboratory and after a few days realized that something in the
dish was killing the bacteria in it. Instead of ignoring it, he set
about analyzing what had happened.

In fact, modern day pharmaceutical companies have realized planning does not always produce the best results, so they
are adding unexpected and random events to their research
protocols, which increase the chances of serendipity being activated.

Serendipity is not magic. What would have happened if
Fleming had simply thrown the dish away? Or if he had been
so tidy that the laboratory was always clean, with no chance of
him leaving a bacteria-filled Petri dish on the table?

Like actors playing an active part in our lives, *serendipity demands that we pay the utmost attention to what is going
on around us, especially to events that are out of the ordinary:*
apparent oversights, errors, seemingly irrelevant opportuni-
ties… maybe they are not irrelevant!

A Highly Productive Visit

Steve Jobs did not discover the visual interfaces for personal computers that are characteristic of Macintosh, but it was his active, curious role that enabled him to acquire the knowledge and ideas. Undoubtedly it also helped to be in the right place at the right time. Several of his colleagues insisted that he visit the Xerox PARC laboratories. They had trouble convincing him because Steve Jobs had absolutely no interest in what they were doing there, but finally he agreed. The technological developments he saw on that visit sparked off a series of connections in his mind, which would forever change the history of computing.

Let the unexpected in

Have you ever said "no" when someone invited you to go on a trip? Has a client asked you to visit their research laboratory, but you declined the offer because you were too busy? Have you been invited to an event or a party on a Friday, but you didn't feel like going?

Maybe you should say "yes" more often, because you never know where the inspiration to awaken your ikigai might be waiting for you.

Serendipity helps to discover things that we didn't know we didn't know. We humans tend to flee from the unknown, we feel safer going around in the same old circles. But if we do not leave our comfort zone, we will never discover the things that we don't even know we don't know.

The key is to create favorable conditions to increase the chances of the unexpected happening. The best way to create serendipity is to give the world signals saying, "Hey, I'm over here, this is me and this is what I like and what I do!"

If you are at home watching television all day, nobody will come to you and nothing will happen. If you go out for a coffee without telling anyone, you will almost certainly end up reading the newspaper alone and most likely nothing will happen.

Creating serendipity requires dynamism. We have to get out and about and be active to provoke situations where the number of things we do not control or have not planned is high enough for the fortunate accident to take place.

3 Paths to serendipity

We can divide the techniques for creating serendipity into three broad categories:

1. *Giving the world signals:* announcing we exist and showing what we think and do.
2. *Adding randomness to our life.*
3. *Getting out and about in the world*—given that the most important thing is to be in the right place at the right time.

Ideas for *giving the world signals* that will help to create serendipity:

- *Publish on social networks.* Fewer than 1% of users create Internet content. If you publish, you are already above the other 99%. Write about what is on your mind, talk about the last film you saw or publish photos of interesting places.
- *Write an e-mail to the author of a book you liked or send a message via social networks to the director of the last movie you saw.* Even if they do not answer you, you are sure to brighten up their day and make them feel grateful! Besides, can you imagine if they do send you a reply?
- *Make yourself a business card*—in Japan it is inconceivable not to have one—and give it to all the people who might be of use for your ikigai. If someone gives you

their card, write them an e-mail the following day.
- *Offer your help to someone you would normally not offer it to.*
- *Ask for help to do something you would normally not need help to do.*

Ideas for adding randomness to your life and increasing the chances of serendipitous events happening:
- *Organize a dinner with a mixture of friends who do not know each other.*
- *Arrange to have a coffee with someone you do not know very well, but that you feel could become a good friend.*
- *Act as a matchmaker between two people who do not know each other,* if you believe there could be good chemistry between them.
- *Organize a party with a surprise theme.*
- If you have an executive position in a company, and want to increase serendipity, *change the surroundings so that the employees interact more.* Create a cafeteria area where the employees will feel comfortable and want to linger longer to chat and swap ideas. Apple built their new corporate headquarters (Apple Park) in the shape of a circle, as we mentioned in the *enso* chapter, in order to make their employees move around through all their departments. Before his death, Steve Jobs asked architects to come up with the best design for increasing "chance meetings" among his employees.
- *Follow people or media on social networks or read webs that talk about things you are normally not interested in.* Outwardly unrelated subjects increase the chances of making creative connections in our mind.
- *Read a book from a genre or on a subject you would never normally read.*

- *Study a new discipline.* Gain access to other knowledge or skills, learn languages or practice different sports. This will increase your chances whenever you find yourself in the right place at the right time.
- *Do something you have never done before.*

Ideas for getting out and about in the world and increasing the chances of being in the right place at the right time:

- *Travel more often.* It is best if you travel with friends or to places where you know people who can introduce you to the local scene.
- On short journeys, *change the car or public transport for walking,* and notice what is around you.
- *Take a different route to work.*
- *Go to a restaurant you have never been to.*

RAK

Random Acts of Kindness

"Random acts of kindness" is a term coined by the writer Anne Herbert in the early eighties to refer to actions that help to raise other people's spirits.

A *RAK* can be something as simple as making someone smile, flattering someone we wouldn't normally speak to, or something involving more of a commitment, like volunteering to help out a community.

The full title of the book written by Anne Herbert and Margaret Paloma Pavel is *Random Kindness and Senseless Acts of Beauty* and it was illustrated by "the Matisse of Japan," Mayumi Oda.

The upside of the bad

Mayumi's illustrations show animals dying under the black rain following the dropping of the bomb on Hiroshima. But little by little, the cats, snakes, rabbits, frogs and fawns get organized, and each of them takes on a small altruistic task that helps the others.

One of them plants a tree, another grows potatoes, others look for food, and the squirrels simply sing and dance at night encouraging the others to start a new life after the nuclear disaster.

The moral of the story is that you do not fight violence and hate with more of the same, but with random acts of beauty and kindness, which achieve the exact opposite of war—making love grow exponentially among people.

> "What you give, you give to yourself.
> What you do not give, you give up."
> ALEJANDRO JODOROWSKY

The greatness of small things

Numerous survey-based investigations have shown that kind people are happier. There is a direct correlation between our level of altruism and our personal satisfaction.

Japan, unfortunately, is a place that is quite used to natural catastrophes. These remind its inhabitants they need to help one another, however small the contribution.

In April 2016, an earthquake devastated several villages in Kumamoto, causing a great loss of life. Our friend Kiyota, a legendary engineer here in Tokyo, decided to leave his job for fifteen days and took the train to Kumamoto. There he set up a stall serving free hot coffee to all those who had been left homeless.

His coffee stand became so popular on social networks, he set up a webpage to collect funds to help the victims and got tens of thousands of euros in a matter of days.

It all started with something as simple as giving away coffee.

Sometimes we overcomplicate life, thinking over how we could fix the world when the answer is to help from the heart by being kind and letting things flow from there.

If you still have not found your ikigai, you can make serving your community your mission.

If you already know what it is, explore how your passion can help to make the world a better place.

Ideas for random acts of kindness

The possibilities are almost infinite—there are as many as there are human needs, but these *RAK* can be used as a starting point for adding a spiritual dimension to your life:

- Smile at the person who serves you in the cafeteria.
- Write a work colleague a note thanking them for any favor they may have done you and leave it on their desk.
- Tell someone how much their new haircut suits them or compliment them on something they are wearing.
- Send an affectionate message to one of those friends with whom, precisely because you are such close friends, you sometimes forget to say how much you love one another.
- Toss a busker a coin.
- Buy your building's caretaker or the office cleaners a tea or a coffee.
- Instead of meeting up with the most popular person in your circle of acquaintances, have a coffee with the shyest one who is most often alone. They need it more than anyone else.
- Forgive someone you fell out with a long time ago.
- Give money to one of the associations you trust.
- Buy a book you liked and make a gift of it to a friend.
- Tell your boss you really like the way they work. Bosses tend not to get praise, only criticism.
- Take a day off and go on an unforgettable outing with a friend or relative who is feeling down.

31st STATION
TOUCH
The importance of touching

How long has it been since you gave a real hug? Have you considered that your body and mind also need such nourishment in order for you to have energy and achieve your aims?

Most of the tribes that still have a natural way of life with a connection to the land know that touch is as important a sense as sight or hearing. *Physical contact with other humans is a vital source of love for nourishing the spirit.*

However, in the West, we are increasingly loath to touch one another. In fact, when thinking about touching another person, many people immediately think in sexual terms.

Perhaps this is because we have learned to brush hands away and keep our distance from the people around us.

"My point is that touch-starvation is not an affliction of the few, but is spiraling outward into the culture of the masses. The awkwardness and inappropriateness of where, how and whom we touch is an issue that affects *everybody*. Whether you are somebody who is unaware that you even *need* touch, or a single man or woman who has been horny for the last fifteen years because you are not in an intimate relationship and the only way you know how to get touch is through sex, or even if you are surrounded by family and children who want to love you and touch you but you don't know how to take it—you *are* affected by touch, or the lack of it.

MARIANA CAPLAN, TO TOUCH IS TO LIVE

An essential sense

The researcher Mariana Caplan (PhD in philosophy, psychology and anthropology) uses scientific data to explain the importance of touching and being touched by others.

Touching is something we learn to love, fear or respect as children. If we are forced to tolerate touching we do not want in our childhood, such as having our cheeks pinched or being made to kiss family acquaintances, we may either become a little averse to touching or, without realizing it, force our children to do the same.

And the reverse is also true; if people were not very affectionate with us when we were children, we will probably feel uncomfortable and insecure touching others.

The Children Of Romania

On the subject of receiving palpable affection, Boris Cyrulnik cites the example of a group of children he treated who were crammed into the orphanages of Romania by the Ceaucescu regime: "Those children were neglected because of a really crazy political philosophy; women were forced to bring children into the world but were incapable of raising them. The orphanages were full to overflowing and nobody took care of those children. They were healthy little things, but the atmosphere was sick, and they were not given the chance to mingle with others, so their physical and psychological development was arrested. They behaved like they were autistic and when we studied them, we saw signs of cerebral atrophy. (...) To begin with, we decided to replace the orphanage with substitute families. After a year, the cerebral atrophy had disappeared. The so-called neuronal resilience had occurred. What happens is that actions like speaking to another person, touching them, feeding them, challenging them or rewarding them stimulate the brain and hormonal secretion."

Learning to touch again

Feeling we are connected to others is vital for our emotional health, which is why it is important to learn to approach others in a friendly, healthy, fear-free fashion. It is not a question of giving out free hugs on the street as was the fashion a few years ago, but of showing affection to the people that matter to us.

People who see touching as something natural have more self-esteem and are calmer. As Caplan says: "When people feel loved as a result of the abundance of touch and affection in their lives, they naturally extend themselves to touch others— be it by a simple pat on the shoulder or a touch of the hand. Secure in themselves, they are open to the other's response, but not expecting it. Their sense of safety and inner stability does not depend on how other people respond to them. They touch in order to express themselves, and so that others may feel cared for."

As part of our map of objectives, it is worth including this point about learning to touch our friends and loved ones again. If we do not feel comfortable at first, we may start with a handshake, a pat on the shoulder or by placing our hand on a loved one's arm.

We will notice immediately not only that we feel better, but that there is gratitude on the face of the person we touch.

Build touching into your life

Touch is one of the most neglected senses, but we can restore it to a prominent place in our life through a series of simple steps:

1. Make a habit of always greeting and saying goodbye to your partner and/or family with a hug and a kiss, however much of a rush you are in.

2. When you are with your partner, regularly take hold of their hand so that your bodies also understand you are united.

3. Make a ritual of greeting friends you have not seen for a long time with a hug.

4. Speak affectionately, appreciatively and gratefully with the people near you. Beautiful words also caress.

UNCERTAINTY

The best plan is not to have one

Imagine that, just for once, you have gotten on a train and have no idea where it is taking you. Close your eyes and imagine yourself in this situation. Which emotions do you feel emerging? Initially, anxiety might appear in the face of the uncertainty, but this feeling is sure to be replaced by the healthy excitement brought on by a new adventure.

Human beings are always caught up in the balancing act of the inner conflict of wanting both freedom and control at the same time. If there is great uncertainty, we get stressed, but when faced by an excess of control, we feel oppressed and want to escape from our routine.

Finding the balancing point between control and uncertainty where we feel comfortable is an important key to self-fulfilment.

The Good Traveler

"I find it funny how all the travel guidebooks in Japanese focus on places to eat," I once said leafing through a guidebook to Hawaii for the Japanese.

"Better than western guidebooks, which only show important buildings and monuments," my workmate Toyoda said to me.

"Ha! You lot only think about eating!"

"If you focus your energy on planning every step of your trip, you won't leave space for making discoveries and getting to know the locals. It's better to travel to enjoy your passions than to go and take photos of the famous sites in all the guidebooks, like they're a list of things to do," explained Toyoda. "My passion is food!"

"The thing about taking photos of famous places is if you're collecting Pokémon is something you guys also do a lot when you travel around Europe," I answered back.

"Ha! You're right. I suppose I'm strange for a Japanese because I like adventure and not planning things. One of my life maxims is Lao-Tze's, "A good traveler has no fixed plans and has no intention of even arriving.""

HÉCTOR

The "who with" is more important than the "where"

Over planning limits our possibilities and may end up making any trip boring, be the trip physical or mental.

An excess of planning can kill the most vibrant passion, whereas uncertainty brings us surprises every day. This is why it is important for spontaneity to guide you in the search for and practice of ikigai.

If you decide to go on a short break, instead of planning every detail of what you are going to see, focus your efforts on deciding who you are going to travel with. Just as with everyday life, *the people who accompany you on your trips are much more important than what you are going to see.*

Your travel companions add to or detract from the experience, so make sure you choose who you go with wisely. It is vital for them to be people who will think like you when it comes to making decisions once you are on your way.

Traveling with a perfect plan is like seeing a movie when you have already read about exactly what is going to happen in each scene. If you wish to embrace adventure and discover new things, buy your plane tickets, book a room for the first night and let yourself be led by your instinct.

Ideas for traveling with ikigai

If you want your trip to be memorable, and an inspiration for your projects, don't try to take in too much. Set yourself a small number of highly motivating objectives. For that, you should seek out the most interesting thing related to the thing that inspires you that can be done in the area.

For example, if you are passionate about astronomy, buy yourself a ticket to Hawaii and plan a visit to the Mauna Kea Observatory, even though you probably have other options closer to home. Talk to the people who work at the observatory and let them guide your trip.

Some advice to match the trip to your passion, not to what the guidebooks dictate:

- Look on the Internet for events going on in your destination that are in line with one of your passions; if you like to dance, look for a dance show; if you like the theater, buy tickets for a performance; if you like photography, join a local group or workshop.

- Stroll around with no route or objective and let yourself be carried along by whatever grabs your attention.
- When in Rome, do as the Romans do. If there are more people walking in one direction than another, go with them and you will probably come across something interesting—a local market, a festival of some kind, religious celebrations...
- Stay at someone's home rather than in hotels. Use any Internet service that allows you to connect with people who make their rooms or homes available for travelers.
- Only book the first plane ticket and the first place to sleep. Leave the rest to chance.
- Join an evening class. It can be anything from a yoga or painting class to a cooking workshop. You will meet local people, and few travelers venture to join classes in the places they travel to. Can you imagine the kind of people you will meet if you spend the evening at a yoga seminar in Anchorage, Alaska?
- Don't worry if things don't work out perfectly. Celebrate it—you will have a good anecdote to tell on your return.

33rd STATION

KAIZEN

Constantly changing for the better

The original meaning of *kaizen* in Japanese was "change for the better." However, after being used in Japanese industry and spreading internationally in the business world after the Second World War, its current meaning could be translated as "continuously change for the better" or "philosophy of continuous improvement."

In most cases of improvement, making a constant effort to meet the target we have set ourselves is more effective than taking a major initiative to try to solve something all at once.

Toyota: *kaizen* laboratory

Toyota was one of the trailblazers in the business world in using *kaizen* to improve its manufacturing processes.

All of this corporation's employees play a part in kaizen, from the factory caretakers up to the members of the board of directors. They all take responsibility when it comes to making decisions that have to do with introducing improvements and eliminating what is known as *muda* ("useless time/elements").

Of course, not only are unneeded processes eliminated. They also consider whether or not eliminating or changing something in the work environment will make it more human.

Decisions are not made lightly, since many factors are taken into consideration when kaizen is applied. One of the keys at Toyota is that they are in no hurry to introduce changes and they analyze everything in detail before changing something.

This way of working has led to them becoming the world's largest automobile company and the one that makes the cars with the lowest rate of manufacturing defects.

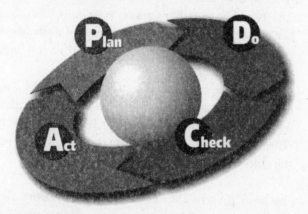

Diagram by Karn G. Bulsuk. Printed under the Creative Commons Attribution 4.0 International License

The PDCA Circle

When it comes to applying kaizen, not just to business but also to our personal life, we may use the "PDCA circle," which stands for Plan, Do, Check and Act.

- The *P for Plan* stage is the time to set concrete objectives and visualize what the future will be like after these objectives have been met. It is also important to describe in detail the steps necessary for the objectives to be met in accordance with what has been planned. On a personal level, this would be the time to sit down and write our New Year's resolutions.

- The *D for Do* stage is there to carry out the plan designed in stage P. It is important to collect data during its execution. On a personal level, this could be something as simple as writing down the days we go to the gym each week on a calendar. If you want to be more detailed, these days you can use all kinds of *Quantified Self devices*, such as smartwatches to gather data on your daily life: the number of paces you have walked, intake of kcals, the time you have spent replying to e-mails, the time you have devoted to project A…
- The *C for Check* stage is aimed at analyzing the data we collected in stage D and comparing the results with what we were hoping for in stage P for Plan. It is the time to reflect on if we have strayed from the plan, if we have met the objectives, and if not, to analyze why.

In his book *Kaizen: The Key to Japan's Competitive Success*, Masaaki Imai stresses the importance of asking yourself questions like these:

o *Why didn't something work as planned?*
o *Why can't we make this process more efficient?*
o *Why did we go to the gym the first two weeks of the year and then stop going?*

We can question ourselves in many different ways. The key is to use the "why" part of the question to uncover the real reason, or what Masaaki Imai calls "the root of the problem." Knowing why something didn't work out as planned is key to being able to introduce changes

- The *A for Act* stage. If what we did in stage D worked well (which we can check in stage C), then in the "acting" stage we will carry on according to what we did in stage D. On the other hand, if things didn't go well in stage D, adjustments must be made.

For example, say our normal routine is to play the piano every morning for half an hour, but in the P (Plan) stage, we instead decide to play for an hour every night after dinner with the aim of preparing ourselves for a concert.

For a month, during stage D (Do), instead of playing the piano in the mornings for half an hour we have done so at night for an hour. At the end of the month we analyze if we have really managed to work better at night than in the morning in stage C (Check) and we ask ourselves:

o *Have we really played for an hour every day or have we failed to do so several times because we were tired at night?*
o *Or maybe we are more nocturnal and there have in fact been several days when we have played for longer than an hour because we felt good and were focused?*

After answering these questions, we return to stage A (Act) and go back to playing the piano for half an hour in the mornings (if the change wasn't positive) or start playing the piano at night if our performance had improved. What we do in stage A from now on becomes our new 'baseline' or 'life standard'.

Negative motivation with kaizen

1. List three concrete changes you need to make in your life—they may be initiatives you have already established in other chapters—but have been putting off for some time.
2. Write a sentence next to each one explaining why you need to make this change come what may. This sen-

tence must be strong enough to act as a lever when it comes to taking the step.

3. You can visualize what your future will be like if you don't take this step in your life. For example, if you choose "doing a sport twice a week" as an improvement, your future visualization sentence could be: "If I don't start to do sports, in ten years' time I'll be visiting the doctor all the time because I'll be suffering from lots of aches and pains." The objective is to activate the change by causing a shock to the system.

1st improvement: _____

_____

What will happen if I don't change in this area?

_____

2nd improvement: _____

_____

What will happen if I don't change in this area?

_____

3rd improvement: _____

_____

What will happen if I don't change in this area?

_____

_____

After a month it is important to analyze whether or not you have kept to the plan and achieved your objectives. If you haven't, don't get frustrated—what is important is to analyze the reason why and look for solutions by creating a new plan with different specific actions to the ones you used a month ago.

Ask yourself these questions:

- After a month, why haven't I managed to make the 1st improvement a reality?

  _____

  _____

- After a month, why haven't I managed to make the 2nd improvement a reality?

  _____

  _____

- After a month, why haven't I managed to make the 3rd improvement a reality?

  _____

  _____

Things not working out as planned doesn't mean failure. Failure, as Einstein said, is to always keep on doing the same thing while expecting different results. If you always do the same thing, nothing will change!

This is a trap we humans very often fall into.

KYUDO
The art of archery

A train is like an arrow shot unerringly at a destination. It always hits the bullseye, like the person who knows what their passion is and decides to throw themselves body and soul into reaching it.

The art of archery, on a symbolic level, has a lot to do with that.

Known as *kyudo* in Japan, this discipline has been practiced since ancient times. In the past, its practice was considered vital both for war and for hunting, and even for preparing the body and mind for everyday life.

It is defined as *an art for exercising the soul,* as we may still observe today in many corners of Japan.

Kyudo exercises the body, mind and spirit at the same time, since it requires large doses of balance, patience, marksmanship and physical and mental stability. That is why the person who practices archery feels capable of calmly facing many situations in their everyday life and sees the world through a prism of serenity and sharpness that many people lack.

Zen and the bow
If the mystical connection between archery and spirituality made it to Europe, it is largely thanks to Eugen Herrigel.

Born in 1885, Herrigel was a professor of philosophy who accepted a job at a Japanese university, attracted by eastern culture and Zen. Once there, he devoted himself to the study of Zen philosophy through learning archery, among other things.

And after many inspirational talks with his master Awa Kenzo, Herrigel was able to put down in writing all that he had learned.

After that, it did not take long for a German publisher to become interested in his paper, which was later translated into many languages, including Japanese. Today, *Zen in the Art of Archery* is still being printed around the world and is considered one of the great modern classics on Japanese culture and Zen philosophy.

In his book, Herrigel reveals to us the secrets of archery and the Zen teachings he learned from his master. With a simplicity that makes him easy to read, the German professor enamored of spiritual Japan explains to us how we may apply this magic connection to everyday life, develop our passion and become masters of our inner peace.

Among other things, Herrigel encourages us to:

- Be patient and allow things to happen in their own good time, without forcing them: "The more obstinately you try to learn how to shoot the arrow for the sake of hitting the goal, the less you will succeed (…). What stands in your way is that you have a much too wilful will."
- Persevere and work every day so that what requires a big effort of us today will later become a fluid and natural response. Practicing kaizen makes that possible.
- Be humble and learn that in order to improve, you must first fail.
- Be flexible and allow your hands to grasp without strangling and your mind to think without getting obsessed.

"Things will no longer harmonize as before. You will see
with other eyes and measure with other measures.
It has happened to me too, and it happens to all who are
touched by the spirit of this art."
EUGEN HERRIGEL,
ZEN IN THE ART OF ARCHERY

A new perspective

Herrigel warns that in the deep study of any art we must be brave and *prepare ourselves to face the world from a new perspective.* All learning and evolution brings with it a change that will force us to see the world from a point of view.

This is what happened to Herrigel when he returned to Europe. Because, as he himself claimed, that is what archery means: *a challenge and a long-haul competition the archer enters into with himself and his spirit,* and an inner evolution that will lead to the path of peace and wisdom.

Although Herrigel would later return to Germany and his public image would be clouded by his support of the Nazis, his teachings have been preserved as a vital source of knowledge of the art of archery and the practice of Zen.

His bow, the very one that enabled him to delve into his own soul and into Buddhist philosophy, may still be admired today in a Kamakura temple, in the Japan he so loved.

"The archer aims at himself"

That was the conclusion Herrigel came to after all the time he spent with his kyudo master. The important thing is not the exterior target, but what is inside the archer that leads them to spiritual perfection.

When you feel you are at conflict—with the world or with yourself—shoot off the following questions like arrows:

1. *How much responsibility do I have for this problem?*
2. *What could I have done better to avoid this situation?*
3. *What mental changes should I make in future to avoid this problem repeating itself?*

TOSHOGU
The lesson of the three monkeys

The final stop on our journey is Nikko, a town to the north of Tokyo which is home to one of the most well-loved and powerful icons of Japanese iconography--the three wise monkeys.

Located above what was once a stable, the wooden sculpture is to be found in the legendary Toshogu Temple. One is covering its ears, another its mouth and the other one its eyes.

The mysterious origin of these emblematic animals may be in a Japanese proverb that states: "See no evil, hear no evil, speak no evil," and which apparently comes from the writings of Confucius. The three wise monkeys have names: Mizaru

(見ざる, the one that does not see), Kikazaru (聞かざる, the one that does not listen) and Iwazaru (言わざる, the one that does not speak). Curiously, the *zaru* ending means both "do not do" and "monkey" in ancient Japanese. This is probably why the proverb was portrayed by a statue with three monkeys back in 1636.

The three filters
Mizaru, Kikazaru and Iwazaru's message concurs with an enlightening story from ancient Greece.

It is said that on one occasion, a disciple came to Socrates's house in a state of agitation and started to talk to him thus:

"Master! I want to tell you how one of your friends has been talking about you maliciously…"

Socrates immediately interrupted him:

"Wait! Did you already examine what you are going to tell me by using the Three Filters test?"

"The Three Filters?" asked the disciple, not knowing what he was talking about.

"Yes," replied Socrates, "The First Filter is TRUTH. Have you carefully examined if what you want to tell me is true in every way?"

"Well no… I heard some neighbors say it."

"But at the very least you must have tested it with the Second Filter, which is KINDNESS. Is it kind at least, this thing you wish to tell me?"

"No, in fact, it is not… It is just the opposite."

"Ah!" rejoined Socrates. "So, let us go on to the last one, the Third Filter. Is it NECESSARY for you to tell me that?"

"In all sincerity, no. It is not necessary."

"So," the sage concluded, "if what you wanted to tell me is neither truthful, kind nor necessary, it would be best if we consign it to oblivion."

So according to Socrates's three filters, before telling someone anything that might have an emotional effect, we have to check how TRUTHFUL, KIND and NECESSARY it is.

Which mental universe do you want to live in?

In fact, Socrates's Three Filters are represented by Iwazaru, the monkey covering its mouth, in the sense of not spreading evil. The person who criticizes or passes on other people's criticism immediately loses potential for awakening their ikigai, since whoever hears them fears—understandably so—that they might be criticized and mocked behind their back.

Pointing out life's negative aspects might be somewhat amusing to those around us, but in the medium and long term, it is not worth it. It cheapens us as humans and makes us less worthy of other people's trust.

By covering its ears, the monkey to its left, Kikazaru, shows us a higher step on our path to spiritual perfection. Besides not passing on negative messages about others, by also refusing to listen to them we avoid our mind being poisoned with unnecessary garbage and preserve the potential we have for good deeds and the awakening of our ikigai.

On the right, Mizaru, the unseeing monkey, shows us not to look at the wrong things, or in the wrong way, which is the definitive step in purifying our filters. Apart from not listening to or passing on negativity, if we also focus our attention —sight and the other senses—on what is useful and beneficial for everyone, starting with ourselves, we will have taken a giant step towards the fulfillment of our dream.

Three Wise Monkeys Exercise

Broadly applying the teachings of Mizaru, Kikazaru and Iwazaru, examine your life and answer these questions:

1. *Do you devote more time to the positive or the negative aspects of life when you watch television or listen to the radio, visit Internet pages or read newspapers?*

   If the latter is the case, replace them with content about culture, technological breakthroughs, psychology or any discipline that may enrich your life.

2. *Do you play along with those who speak ill of others in your conversations with other people?*

   If this is so, then to clean your mind of "trash," which makes you neither better nor more effective, try to bring the conversation around to other topics. With time, the "fault-finder" will realize you are not a recipient for their diatribe and will seek out other accomplices.

3. *Do you help others to develop their best qualities when speaking with them?*

If you don't do this yet, you should realize that other people are your mirror and so the help and recognition you give them is something you also give to yourself.

The Three Wise Monkeys at Toshogu Temple. Photo by Ray from Manila. Printed under the Creative Commons Attribution 2.0 Generic license.

How to Awaken the Power of Ikigai

Tune in to your life goals

We can spend days, months and years wrapped up in our routines, ensnared by our mundane responsibilities. However, as time goes by, we will ask ourselves if we are really living our life or just getting by to meet other people's expectations.

When was the last time you stopped to think what your mission in life is?

For this final exercise, make yourself a cup of tea or your favorite herbal brew and sit down with a pen and paper. Take your time about it--there is no rush. You probably have lots of things to do: chores, work, going to the supermarket, planning this weekend's trip...but what can be more important than tuning in to your ikigai?

What you are going to do now is important, so put aside all that stuff that is keeping you busy and allow yourself to carry out this final exercise, which may give your life a new direction.

You are going to build the compass which will help you travel in step with your ikigai.

In future, whenever you find yourself feeling lost, you can always come back to it to get back on course.

The four components of ikigai

Our current society is designed to orient our actions and thoughts to earning money, that is, to invest our energy in the lowest part of the Venn diagram.

However, if we do not take the other components of the ikigai diagram into account, and only focus on continuously earning money, our entire life can become empty of meaning.

Our objective in this final exercise, after our journey together through thirty-five stations, is to merge the four components so that our life is at one with our values and goals.

In order to do that, we suggest you divide a sheet of paper into four parts:

1. What I love	2. What the world needs.
3. What I can be paid for	4. What I am good at

We shall start to write in the upper left quadrant.

1. What I love

This is the easiest part of the exercise. Make a note of everything you can think of that makes you feel good or happy. Write quickly, without overthinking it. Be completely honest and only write down what you are passionate about.

Do you like sleeping under the stars? Write it! Are you happy when cooking a new dish? Write it! Don't judge if it is something that society considers good and useful. The objective is for you to write everything that makes you happy.

End each sentence with "_____
makes me happy."

2. What the world needs

If we aim to spend most of our time doing the things we love, our feeling of happiness will grow, but we run the risk of falling into the pit of selfishness.

One of the secrets to a long and healthy life that the elderly people of Okinawa taught us is that they all belong to communities, to a *Moai* where they help one another. Feeling we are useful to those around us is one of the secrets to self-fulfillment as human beings.

So, in this second quadrant write what others need – not just your friends and family, but the world too.

You may begin each sentence with *"My beloved _____ needs _____."*

Then you can write *"The world needs _____ "* or more specific things like *"My colleagues need _____ "* or *"My kids' school needs _____."*

3. What I can be paid for

If we confine ourselves to following what we have written in the first two quadrants, we may be happy and feel we are useful to others, but we still need to make a living and have money for our projects.

One of the first things we noticed when we were living with the elderly people of Ogimi in Okinawa was that most of them still had some kind of business, even at the age of eighty or ninety. For example, they sold the vegetables grown in their orchards in the local market or, in the case of Yuki, the leather bags and wallets she made herself at the age of ninety-three.

We should not feel at all ashamed to ask for money in exchange for what we know how to do. Getting financial gain from what you are good at will allow you to lead a well-balanced professional-personal life.

There are things that make us money directly and others that have the potential to do so in the future. One of the keys to prosperity, mentioned by role models such as Warren Buffett, is to learn to think long term and anxiety free.

In the third part of this exercise, you may record what makes you money right now, without judging whether or not it makes you happy. Confine yourself to writing "Now I make a living by _____."

Next, write down other possible sources of income that could sustain you in the future, with phrases like "In the future I would like to earn money by _____."

4. What I am good at

Sometimes it is hard for us to know what we are good at because our potential has been shrouded by past emotional experiences. For example, if we had a bad math or music teacher, we will probably end up saying to ourselves things like: "I'm no good at math" or "Music's not for me."

We often block our aspirations simply because we decided "we're no good at it" or because others made us believe that was so. But the reality is we humans can do anything we want to.

And who better than yourself to know what your talent is?

Leave aside what others might have told you and write here what you yourself honestly believe. Begin your sentences in this quadrant of the sheet with *"I'm good at _____*

_____."

In addition to the virtues you have right here and now, review those skills you could develop if you get the necessary preparation.

"In the future I can be good at _____ if I prepare myself by doing _____."

At this point, your compass with the four ikigai components should look like this:

Héctor's example of the four *ikigai* components

1. What I love	2. What the world needs
Writing makes me happy	My friend Alfredo needs me to listen to him more because he's just lost his job
Traveling with friends and family makes me happy	
Going to the movies makes me happy	My family need me to spend more time with them
Playing videogames makes me happy	
Having coffee makes me happy	My colleagues need me to sit down more with each of them and help them
Reading makes me happy	
Chatting to the people I love makes me happy	My friends Pepe and Juan need to see more of me and need me to tell them more often how important they are to me
Going for walks makes me happy	
Taking photos makes me happy	
Listening to music makes me happy	My readers need more affection from me and not just books and Internet webs
Any creative task makes me happy	
Programming computers makes me happy	The world needs more love and less hate
	The world needs more altruism

3. What I can be paid for	4. What I am good at
Now I make a living by:	Right now I am good at:
Working at a multinational in Tokyo	Programming computers
In the future I would like to:	Ordering and summing up many sources of information
Use part of my savings to set up the online business I've had in mind for years but don't dare to take the big step to do	Writing nonfiction
	Taking photos
Write more books	In the future I would like to be good at:
Sell my photographs	Writing fiction
Be a speaker on Japanese culture	Running my own business
Invest the money I have now in reliable financial assets	Doing yoga
	Composing music

Take action

If you have gotten this far and have filled in the four quadrants on the sheet, congratulations! You carry within you the seed of success.

In this second part of the exercise, you are going to commit to taking a series of decisions that will set your ikigai in motion.

Taking action instead of being mere spectators is the key to getting our ikigai to emerge from inside us.

There is the false belief that our purpose in life is something magical we are destined to find accidentally or through a revelation. However, when you listen carefully to the stories of people who have found their passion, you realize it was not down to coincidence or the work of magic. It was perseverance and tenacity that, with time, led to them being good at something and developing a passion for it.

They often had to try many things through trial and error until they found their *ikigai*. In other cases, at an early age they found something that over time became their source of income and their passion. Action comes before passion.

ACTION ➡ PASSION

Or, as Donald Kendall said, "The only place where Success comes before Work is in the dictionary."

You can *take action* in many ways, like sending that e-mail you have been wanting to write for weeks, starting painting classes, changing your job if you don't like your current one, getting married if you are really in love, getting divorced if your relationship has been dead for years, going on that trip you have always dreamed about…

The fundamental thing is to do it. *You do not need anyone's permission—it is your life.*

Now go back to the sheet with the four ikigai components and underline whatever you have not been devoting enough time to recently. That is, things which are important to you, but you have lately been sidelining.

Write a list for each of these neglected things with three specific actions you will undertake from now on, to get the forgotten aspects of your life up and running and awaken your ikigai.

Following on from the previous exercise that we included as a guide, if for example I already know how to play an instrument and want to be good at composing music, I may start

by...
- *Listening again to the pieces and songs that most move me.*
- *Learning one of them on the piano or another instrument to understand its harmony.*
- *Composing a melody of my own based on this exercise.*

Change your heading when necessary

If you notice a prevailing sense of dissatisfaction, and that you are brooding over problems all day long, look at the four quadrants again and ask yourself: am I including the four ikigai components in my everyday life? Am I only devoting myself to making money? Am I allocating enough time to my passions?

These moments of doubt encourage us to make decisions, get rid of things that do not work and take up other activities.

If we feel it is time to change tack, we might feel afraid at first, but once we have corrected our direction, we will realize that the fear of change was much greater than the change itself.

Forget about what no longer inspires you and write new ideas in your quadrants. Ikigai, like life itself, is not something fixed or immovable. Change your direction if you need to! Life is too short to be stuck in a desert.

Get rid of unnecessary stuff or take new actions, but do not stand still. Nothing new or exciting will happen if you do not take steps to make it happen.

The end is the beginning

On this page one journey ends and another begins.

We have passed through thirty-five stations together and each one of them has provided us with a practical tool to discover, strengthen and accomplish our life goals.

The course ends here but this is when the most important thing begins. When you close this book, after reviewing the thirty-five keys, your adventure begins.

Pursuing your passion and developing it to be shared with others is the greatest objective a human being can hope to achieve in their future.

We take our leave with a few last lines to wish you a *bon voyage*.

Thanks for coming with us this far.
If you employ some of these tools in your life,
you will undoubtedly achieve transcendental changes
which will enable you to enhance your ikigai
and reach your goals.

However, do not make the mistake of taking
your objectives too seriously.
Go after them with a permanent smile,
allowing margin for error and learning on the way,
with others and with yourself.
Wherever you may be and whatever you may accomplish,
always remember that everything is still to be done
and everything is in your hands.
HÉCTOR GARCIA (KIRAI) & FRANCESC MIRALLES

The 35 keys to living your ikigai

1. If you aim to improve by 10%, consider what you need to do to improve by 100%.
2. Include at least one 'impossibility' in your day-to-day agenda.
3. Practice patience and perseverance with what you have resolved to do.
4. Devote 21 days to implementing a positive, new habit.
5. Ask people you trust for feedback on what you are doing.
6. Seek out a mentor who can guide you in your passion.
7. Imitate and improve on what you like for your next project.
8. Identify what you don't like in order to discover, through a process of elimination, what you do.
9. Each week develop a virtue you want to strengthen.
10. Share your passion with like-minded people to learn and improve together.
11. Get out of your comfort zone and explore new territories.
12. Prioritize important things ahead of urgent ones.
13. Push aside what is neither essential nor worthwhile in your life.
14. Baptize your project with a name that may spur you into action.
15. Recover your childhood values and dreams.
16. Motivate yourself by recalling your life's "greatest hits."
17. Recognize your "level one" friends and give them the attention they deserve.

18. Join the dots from your past to understand your present.
19. Establish a screen-free and virtual life-free time slot.
20. Make "slow life" a part of your meals and leisure time.
21. Do just one thing at a time, without getting side-tracked.
22. Write something personal for at least 5 minutes each day.
23. Take up the art of *haiku* to get to know your emotions.
24. Take the crucial decisions you need at this time in your life.
25. "Sleep on" the questions you still have no answer to.
26. Flow by drawing the *enso* circle.
27. Solve a *koan* each week.
28. Practice giving your undivided attention to your every-day activities.
29. Let yourself be carried along by the serendipities and other coincidences of your life.
30. Carry out an altruistic act of kindness every day.
31. Hug your loved ones regularly.
32. Occasionally travel without a destination and allow yourself to be surprised.
33. Make *kaizen* part of the awakening of your *ikigai*.
34. Always aim the arrow of improvement at yourself.
35. Distance yourself from the sources of negativity.

ACKNOWLEDGEMENTS

To our family and friends for always being there,
come what may.

To Sandra Bruna and her team,
for always making the impossible possible.

To Carol, L, editor, exceptional documentalist and friend.
To Vicente, Rosa, Carlos and Rodrigo,
for their affectionate final review.

To the publishers all over the world who are spreading the
ikigai philosophy through our book.

To the booksellers, for making their passion
into an exercise in shared wisdom.

To all our readers, for their inspiring support and affection.

The Tuttle Story
"Books to Span the East and West"

Our core mission at Tuttle Publishing is to create books which bring people together one page at a time. Tuttle was founded in 1832 in the small New England town of Rutland, Vermont (USA). Our fundamental values remain as strong today as they were then—to publish best-in-class books informing the English-speaking world about the countries and peoples of Asia. The world has become a smaller place today and Asia's economic, cultural and political influence has expanded, yet the need for meaningful dialogue and information about this diverse region has never been greater. Since 1948, Tuttle has been a leader in publishing books on the cultures, arts, cuisines, languages and literatures of Asia. Our authors and photographers have won numerous awards and Tuttle has published thousands of books on subjects ranging from martial arts to paper crafts. We welcome you to explore the wealth of information available on Asia at **www.tuttlepublishing.com**.

Published by Tuttle Publishing, an imprint of Periplus Editions (HK) Ltd.
www.tuttlepublishing.com

Copyright©2017 by Héctor García and Francesc Miralles
Originally published in Spanish as *El Método Ikigai: Despierta Tu Verdadera Pasión y Cumple Tus Propósitos Vitales* by Penguin Random House Grupo Editorial, S.A.U., Barcelona, 2017.

Translation rights arranged by Sandra Bruna Agencia Literaria, SL.
All rights reserved.

Translation copyright © 2020 by Periplus Editions (HK) Ltd.

Distributed by

North America, Latin America & Europe
Tuttle Publishing
364 Innovation Drive
North Clarendon, VT 05759-9436 U.S.A.
Tel: (802) 773-8930; Fax: (802) 773-6993
info@tuttlepublishing.com
www.tuttlepublishing.com

Asia Pacific
Berkeley Books Pte. Ltd.
3 Kallang Sector
#04-01, Singapore 349278
Tel: (65) 6741-2178; Fax: (65) 6741-2179
inquiries@periplus.com.sg
www.tuttlepublishing.com

TUTTLE PUBLISHING® is a registered trademark of Tuttle Publishing, a division of Periplus Editions (HK) Ltd.

Originally published ISBN: 978-4-8053-1599-6

This edition ISBN: 978-0-8048-5533-4 for sale in the Indian Subcontinent only

Library of Congress publication data is in progress.

Printed and bound in India by Thomson Press India Ltd.
23 22 21 20   10 9 8 7 6 5 4 3 2 1